D0722772

THE KOREAN WAR

CHRONICLE OF AMERICA'S WARS

Ruth Tenzer Feldman

↳ LERNER PUBLICATIONS COMPANY
MINNEAPOLIS

COLUSA COUNTY FREE LIBRARY

Introduction: Tracer bullets and flares streak through the sky during a Second Infantry battle in North Korea.

Chapter 1: Citizens in Russian-occupied North Korea carry a portrait of the Russian leader Stalin in a local parade.

Chapter 2: South Korean women search for relatives killed during battle in Seoul.

Chapter 3: U.S. Marines newly arrived in Pusan load into trucks to move into the battle zone.

Chapter 4: Tanks and troops move to the front, north of the 38th Parallel, in October 1950.

Chapter 5: Marines take a break as they fight their way southeast from the Chosin Reservoir to the Sea of Japan.

Chapter 6: General Douglas MacArthur inspects troops during a tour of the Korean battlefront.

Chapter 7: Officials from the United States and North Korea look over maps showing the northern and southern boundaries of the demilitarized zone during the Panmunjom truce talks.

Epilogue: Canadian officers of the UN forces in Korea read about the truce.

Copyright © 2004 by Ruth Tenzer Feldman

All rights reserved. International copyright secured. No part of this book may be reproduced, stored in a retrieval system, or transmitted in any form or by any means—electronic, mechanical, photocopying, recording, or otherwise—without the prior written permission of Lerner Publications Company, except for the inclusion of brief quotations in an acknowledged review.

For my sister, Judith, who shared the Korean War with me, and for my brother, Stuart, who was yet to be born.

Lerner Publications Company
A division of Lerner Publishing Group
241 First Avenue North
Minneapolis, MN 55401

Website address: www.lernerbooks.com

Library of Congress Cataloging-in-Publication Data

Feldman, Ruth Tenzer.
    The Korean War / by Ruth Tenzer Feldman.
      p.   cm. — (Chronicle of America's wars)
    Includes bibliographical references and index.
    Contents: Korea sometime in January 1951—Drawing the line—Storm!—Saving the South—North to the Yalu almost—"An entirely new war"—Setting limits—The talking war—Epilogue—Timeline.
    ISBN: 0-8225-4716-3 (lib. bdg. : alk. paper)
    1. Korean War, 1950–1953—Juvenile literature. [1. Korean War, 1950–1953.] I. Title. II. Series.
DS918.F397 2004
951.904'2—dc21   2002156557

Manufactured in the United States of America
1 2 3 4 5 6 – JR – 09 08 07 06 05 04

TABLE OF CONTENTS

INTRODUCTION

Korea—Sometime in January 1951.

It was bitterly cold that night. Sitting in her farmhouse in a small village near Hongchon, an old woman calmly smoked a long-stemmed clay pipe. That evening she had made steamed rice and pickled vegetables for Chung Dong-kyu and other soldiers in the South Korean army. Their mission was simple: spy on North Korean soldiers and report their movements to the U.S. forces. *Namu-jike,* which means "wood A-frame," was the South Korean's password that night. At midnight everything was quiet.

Suddenly, the night sky exploded with gunfire. North Koreans had captured the sentry guarding the village. They forced the password from him. Then they tricked some South Korean soldiers into coming out of hiding and killed them.

Chung knew he was no longer safe in the farmhouse. He and two others ran to the old woman's tiny barn.

A North Korean soldier called to the old woman in the farmhouse. He asked her if there were any South Korean soldiers nearby. She didn't move. She said nothing.

Chung thought that the old woman acted this way because "living so close to the 38th Parallel had caused her to see northern and southern soldiers take and retake her village many times. She showed neither surprise nor fear over the fact of the latest changeover."

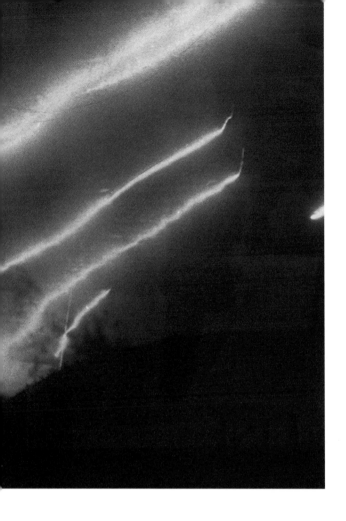

When he referred to the 38th Parallel, Chung meant the line on the map that marks 38 degrees north latitude. Mapmakers divide our planet into sections using lines of longitude and latitude. Latitude lines circle the globe north and south of the equator, which is at 0 degrees latitude. The 38th Parallel line that divides Korea also runs through Charlottesville in Virginia, Stockton in California, and is about 150 miles north of Tokyo, Japan.

EYEWITNESS QUOTE:

"We . . . lay down. It was very dark. . . . Our hiding place smelled foul, and we soon discovered that we had bedded ourselves down in . . . ox dung. There was nothing we could do, and no time to do it, for a pair of North Korean soldiers swinging the muzzles of their automatic rifles soon appeared in the yard."

—Chung Dong-kyu (Donald K. Chung)

The 38th Parallel was so important to Korea that millions of people—including U.S. soldiers and other UN troops—were wounded or killed in Korea as armies crossed it over and over again.

After the old woman said nothing to the North Korean soldier, he shouted at her, repeating his question. "Are there any South Korean soldiers nearby?" She looked at him firmly and lied. "I haven't seen any!"

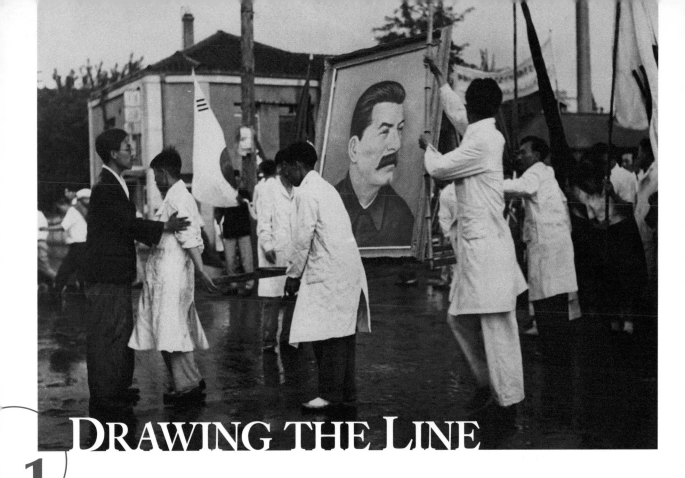

DRAWING THE LINE

Korea is a peninsula of land that sticks out of China toward the islands of Japan. It is mainly mountainous, except along the western coast. Winds from the south in summer bring heat and humidity. The winter winds blow from the north to bring freezing cold, especially in the mountains. In 1910 Japan occupied Korea and took control of the country. It was still under Japanese occupation when World War II (1939–1945) ended.

One of the United States' allies in World War II had been the Union of Soviet Socialist Republics, or Soviet Union for short. During World War II, the Soviet Union joined the European Allies in fighting against Hitler after German troops invaded, but it had not declared war on Japan, another enemy of the Allies. After the Allies won the European part of the war with the help of the Soviet Union, they asked the Soviet Union to help fight in Asia.

On August 8, 1945, the Soviet Union declared war on Japan. Soviet leader Joseph Stalin sent forces against Japanese troops occupying Manchuria, a mountainous area just north of the nation of Korea. The Soviets then prepared to enter Korea to fight the Japanese there.

U.S. troops were busy battling the Japanese elsewhere in Asia. Military leaders in the United States were concerned that the Soviets might try to occupy Korea and turn it into a Communist state, too. They decided to divide Korea between Soviet troops and U.S. troops, so that the Soviets would not gain control of the entire country.

North and South Korea after 1953

RUSSIA

CHINA

MANCHURIA

Yalu R.

Yalu R.

Changjin R.

Chosin Reservoir

Unjong

Sinuiju

Unsan

Chongchon R.

Hungnam

NORTH KOREA

Wonsan

⊛ Pyongyang

DEMILITARIZED ZONE (DMZ)

Haeju

Panmunjom

Kaesong

38th Parallel

Kimpo

Hongchon

Seoul

Hoengsong

Inchon

Osan

Han R.

SEA OF JAPAN

KOREA BAY

YELLOW SEA

Kum R.

Taejon

Sangju

Kunsan

Taegu

SOUTH KOREA

Pusan

Korean Strait

JAPAN

N

Miles
0   25   50   75   100

0   50   100   150
Kilometers

On August 10, 1945, two young colonels in the U.S. Army, Dean Rusk and Charles Bonesteel, were studying a basic map of the country. They noticed that the line marking 38 degrees north latitude (the 38th Parallel) split Korea into about two equal parts.

The United States suggested to Joseph Stalin that Soviet forces occupy Korea from its northern border with Manchuria south to the 38th Parallel. U.S. forces would occupy Korea from the 38th Parallel south to the tip of the Korean peninsula. Each army would take charge of the Japanese troops and Korean people in its part of the country.

The United States dropped two atomic bombs on Japan in early August 1945. The death and destruction caused by these bombs brought a new threat to world peace. On August 14, Japan agreed to surrender.

But World War II was over. Although Koreans had a long and proud history, Japan had controlled the country for thirty-five years. When their Japanese rulers left, Korea had no government, no police force, no army. Instead of having one occupying army (the Japanese), Koreans were faced with two—the Soviets and the United States.

THE FIRST FRACTURE

The United States and the Soviet Union agreed to occupy and maintain order in Korea until Koreans on both sides of the dividing line could be reunited into a single, independent country. Great Britain and China agreed to join an official committee to oversee occupation of Korea. But the committee failed to agree on how northern and southern Korea would be reunited.

In 1945 the ceremony marking the surrender of Japanese forces in South Korea took place in the Government Building in the capital city of Seoul.

On November 14, 1947—more than two years after Korea was divided—the newly formed United Nations (UN) decided to take on the problem. The UN agreed to help the Koreans establish their own government. The new Korean government would be made up of people elected by secret ballot, similar to elections in the United States. After the Koreans established their government, all foreign troops would leave the country.

But the Soviet Union refused to go along with the plan. Free elections could mean that they would lose control of the area they occupied. The Soviet Union sealed off the northern half of Korea and refused to let UN commissioners carry out elections there. So on May 10, 1948, Koreans held elections only in the south. They elected a national assembly, which established the Republic of Korea (ROK) on August 15, 1948. Syngman Rhee became president. Rhee was a wealthy, well-educated man who had spent most of his life in the United States. More than half of the people elected to the national assembly came from political parties that opposed Rhee's views. Some groups in the country

Syngman Rhee

rebelled against the new leadership, but they failed to overthrow Rhee.

Over the next two years, the people of the new republic—also called South Korea—began to build a nation. The United States withdrew most of its forces but left behind military advisers to help train South Korea's new army.

Shortly after the Republic of Korea was formed, the Soviet Union started a separate government in northern Korea. The government was led by Kim Il Sung, a military leader who had been trained in the Soviet Union and fought against the Japanese in Manchuria. Kim was also head of the Korean Workers' Party, a Communist political group similar to the Communist Party that ruled the Soviet

The United Nations

After World War II, the countries that had fought against Germany and Japan met to discuss how to prevent a war like it from happening again. They worked out the Charter of the United Nations. In June 1945, fifty countries signed the charter, and the United Nations was established on October 24, 1945, with headquarters in New York City. Over the years, more than one hundred other nations have joined the organization. The four purposes of the United Nations are (1) to preserve world peace and security; (2) to encourage nations to be just in their actions toward each other; (3) to help nations cooperate in solving their problems, and; (4) to serve as the organization through which countries can reach these goals. A major part of the United Nations is the International Court of Justice. Many committees, such as UNICEF (United Nations Children's Fund) and UNHCR (Office of the United Nations High Commissioner for Refugees), bring aid to groups around the world.

Union. Kim formed the Democratic People's Republic of Korea—also called North Korea. At first, Kim was popular with many North Koreans. Then he and the Korean Workers' Party took control of elections, newspapers, and radio and moved farmers from their own land onto government-owned farms. About one million North Koreans fled to South Korea.

Most Soviet troops left North Korea, but some remained. Soviets equipped the North Korean army with combat planes, tanks, and heavy weapons, and they trained the North Koreans to use them.

COLD WAR JITTERS

While all this was going on in Korea, political changes were taking place in China—Korea's mighty neighbor. Japan had also occupied China during World War II. When Japanese troops left in 1945, two political groups fought to control China. One group, the Nationalists, was led by Chiang Kai-shek. The other group, the Communists, was led by Mao Zedong.

Mao Zedong

U.S. soldiers stayed in China until 1947. The United States backed the Chinese Nationalists, in the hope that the Nationalists would establish a successful democratic government. But Chiang's party failed to bring about needed economic and political reforms. The Communists meanwhile gained in military strength and in popularity. After U.S. troops left, China erupted into civil war. By October 1949, the Nationalists had fled to the tiny island of Taiwan (also called Formosa), about one hundred miles off the coast of mainland China. The Communists controlled the rest of China.

Communism was spreading elsewhere, too. The Soviet Union continued to force its political system on countries in Eastern Europe. Countries such as Poland and Hungary soon had Communist

Kim's Song

During the election in the Soviet-controlled northern half of Korea in 1948, pictures of presidential candidate Kim Il Sung *(right)* and Soviet leader Joseph Stalin hung side by side. The words of one song, praising candidate Kim were:

Snow-bound Manchurian plain, tell me,
Long, long forest night, let me ask you.
Who is the unwavering partisan?
Who is the peerless patriot?
Ah, ah, his name is one we long to hear—our general.
Ah, ah, his name is brilliant—General Kim Il Sung.

Senator Joseph McCarthy and the House Un-American Activities Committee investigated Communism in many parts of American life. Fear of Communism was sweeping the United States at that time.

governments. The United States and the Soviet Union became involved in a Cold War, a struggle for power around the world.

Just about the time the Communists took over China, an U.S. spy mission discovered that the Soviets were testing a nuclear device. From 1945 to 1949, the United States was the only country that had the atomic bomb. Now it looked as though the Soviet Union had one as well.

Fear of Communism swept over the United States. Some Americans blamed President Harry Truman for "losing China" to the Communists. In Congress the House Un-American Activities Committee started looking for Communists inside the U.S. government. Joseph McCarthy, a senator from Wisconsin, claimed that there were

Communists in the state department, the entertainment industry, and the military.

President Truman and his advisers faced many difficult questions. They worried about the Soviets and the atomic bomb. They looked for ways to stop the spread of Communism in Europe by the Soviet Union and in Asia by China. They studied mistakes the United States made in China and debated ways to avoid similar mistakes in Korea. They analyzed where in Europe and Asia to send U.S. troops to help countries "draw the line" on Communism. They discussed the differences between Rhee's government in the southern part of Korea and Kim's government in the north. The decisions that the president and his advisers came up with shaped their plan for reuniting Korea.

FAST
FACT

KOREAN NAMES

In China and Korea, a person's family name comes first, followed by other names. For example, Kim Il Sung's family name is Kim, and his first name is Il Sung. Syngman Rhee is an exception. Having spent many years in the United States, he Americanized his name.

MIXED SIGNALS

The United States responded to the problems in Asia in a way that sent mixed signals to Korea, China, and the Soviet Union. Under a program called the Truman Doctrine, the United States gave money and military aid to countries in Europe as a way to prevent the spread of Soviet-style Communism there. Even though Soviet-backed Communists controlled North Korea, the United States gave very little military aid to the Republic of Korea in the south. President Rhee boasted that with modern military weapons, he could get rid of the Communist government in North Korea in two weeks. Fearing that Rhee might provoke the Soviets into starting World War III, the United States didn't want to take the chance by giving Rhee the weapons he wanted.

In January 1950, U.S. Secretary of State Dean Acheson gave a speech that listed places in Asia where the United States would actively defend against Communism. He left out Taiwan and Korea. About the same time, U.S. warships sailed into the waters between mainland China and Taiwan, but not into Korean waters. Kim Il Sung knew about

President Harry Truman asks Congress for funds to aid countries fighting the spread of Communism.

Acheson's speech and the U.S. warships. He decided that the United States was sending a signal to North Korea. Kim Il Sung thought the speech meant that the United States would try to stop the Communist Chinese from attacking Taiwan. But it would not try to stop the Communist North Koreans from attacking South Korea. Both Mao and Stalin agreed with the way Kim read the signals from the United States.

During the spring of 1950, U.S. spies reported that North Korea was preparing to attack South Korea. They had seen a few North Korean soldiers crossing the 38th Parallel into South Korea several times. Most U.S. military officers, however, thought that the North Koreans only wanted to stir up trouble and steal food from the prosperous South. They called the North Korean activities "rice raids."

U.S. forces in the region were commanded by General Douglas MacArthur. He had been a great hero in World War II. After the war, he took charge of establish-

EYEWITNESS QUOTE:

"War is no longer rationally a means of settling international problems. . . . Both sides lose. . . . That is the basic reason for my belief that war is not on the doorstep."

—General Douglas MacArthur

ing a new government in Japan, while U.S. troops occupied the country under the terms of surrender. MacArthur had his headquarters in Japan and rarely went to Korea. But he was certain that North Korea would not dare to start a war that might bring in the powerful United States.

North Korea's actions continued to worry the Joint Chiefs of Staff (the highest military advisers to the U.S. president). On June 20, 1950, Omar Bradley, the head of the Joint Chiefs, asked General MacArthur whether a major invasion of South Korea would happen soon. MacArthur still said he didn't think so. But even as he spoke, small groups of North Korean soldiers were sneaking deep inside South Korea.

General Douglas MacArthur

STORM!

2

On Saturday night, June 24, 1950, many South Korean soldiers and their U.S. military advisers had left their posts. Some were in Japan for a relaxing weekend. Others partied at the new officer's club in Seoul, the capital of South Korea. Estimates show that only about one-third of South Korea's ninety-five thousand troops were on duty or in their barracks that night.

During that night, about ninety thousand North Korean troops advanced toward the 38th Parallel. Perhaps as many as forty-five thousand other soldiers remained on high alert in North Korea. By 4:00 A.M. on Sunday, just as the mountains grew visible in the dawn sky, a code word was sent to every North Korean army division: Storm!

North Korea attacked at four points along the 38th Parallel. Most of the troops headed for Seoul, only thirty miles away. The advancing North Korean army included 150 huge Soviet-made T-34 tanks, one of the mightiest tanks of World War II.

South Korean soldiers rushed to return to duty, but they faced the massive invasion without tanks of their own. Their anti-tank guns and bazookas (small rocket launchers) were useless against the tough T-34s. By the next day, much of South Korea's army had been destroyed.

THE UNITED STATES RESPONDS

The U.S. embassy in Seoul sent a telegram about the invasion to the State Department in Washington, D.C. Secretary of State Dean Acheson telephoned President Truman, who was vacationing at home in Independence, Missouri. Truman

They Started It!

North Korea invaded South Korea at 4:00 A.M. on June 25, 1950. At 9:30 A.M., North Korean president Kim Il Sung came on the radio with this message:

> The South Korean puppet clique [government] has rejected all methods for peaceful reunification proposed by the Democratic People's Republic of Korea [North Korea] and has dared to commit armed aggression against the Haeju district north of the 38th Parallel. The Democratic People's Republic of Korea has ordered a counterattack to repel the invading troops. The South Korean puppet clique will be held responsible for whatever results may be brought about by this development.

This was a lie. South Korea had not invaded Haeju district. But at 11:00 A.M. that day, North Korea officially declared war against South Korea.

was furious. He was sure that the Soviet Union was behind the attack.

Truman rushed back to Washington to meet with military and political advisers. At the same time, the U.S. delegate, or representative, to the United Nations urged the member countries of the UN to help. South Korea was a new member of the UN. North Korea was not a UN member, since it had not allowed the UN to monitor its elections.

The United Nations' efforts to preserve peace are directed by the Security Council. But if one of the permanent members of the council vetoes (votes against) an action to keep the peace, the UN cannot under-

take that action. The Soviet Union supported North Korea. It could have vetoed any resolution to assist South Korea. But at this time, the Soviet Union had withdrawn its delegate from UN meetings. It was protesting the fact that the UN would not grant membership to Communist China. With no Soviet delegate on the Security Council to veto their decision, the council voted to demand that North Korea withdraw its troops from areas south of the 38th Parallel.

Meanwhile, North Korean troops closed in on Seoul. South Korean troops rushed to defend their country's capital, which was in chaos. The South Korean army blew up the Han River bridge in the middle of Seoul. Some say that they destroyed it to prevent the North Koreans from crossing after the South Korean army was safely across, but the bridge blew up too early. Others say that the bridge was blown up to stop South Korean troops from retreating southward. In either case, more than five hundred people—soldiers and civilians—were on the bridge when it exploded.

President Truman ordered General MacArthur to evacuate U.S. civilians from the U.S. embassy in Seoul. More than two thousand U.S. citizens and other non-Koreans were taken to safety in Japan. On

THE UN SECURITY COUNCIL

The main objective of the UN Security Council is to preserve and enforce peace. The council is made up of five permanent members including the United States and Russia and six members that are elected for two-year terms.

FAST FACT

June 27, Truman ordered military supplies to be sent to South Korea and planes sent to protect South Korean troops and supply movements.

The North Korean army was swift and powerful. On June 28, Seoul fell to the Communists. MacArthur flew to Korea the next day. He reported that the North Korean army would soon take over all of South Korea. So on June 30, Truman ordered U.S. troops into South Korea and ordered U.S. planes to attack military bases in the North. He also ordered U.S. war-ships to set up a blockade along the Korean coast and to bombard North Korean positions.

FAST FACT

BLOCKADES

In a naval blockade, ships are anchored off an enemy port city to prevent enemy ships from entering or leaving the city. A blockade also prevents supply ships from bringing needed supplies for the military and for civilians to the enemy port.

The U.S. troops closest to Korea were stationed in Japan. They were part of a peacetime army of occupation. Many of the soldiers there lacked up-to-date weapons and combat experience. They were suddenly faced with war.

The first U.S. troops to fight against the North Koreans were in Task Force Smith, a group of about 540 men under the command of Lieutenant Colonel Charles (Brad) Smith. They landed in Pusan, the southernmost city in South Korea, and headed north up the main road toward Seoul. Their job was to block the advance of the North Korean army until more troops arrived at Pusan.

Task Force Smith stopped near Osan, about twenty-eight miles south of Seoul. They spread out on three hills overlooking the narrow highway from Seoul to Pusan and set up six howitzers (field cannons). They waited. Morale was high. Some of the men thought the North Koreans would run away at the sight of U.S. soldiers.

"Hey, Lieutenant, look over there," Sergeant Loren Smith said to Lieutenant Phil Day on the hot, rainy morning of July 5. "Can you believe? Those are T-34 tanks, sir, and I don't think they're going to be friendly toward us."

Coming down the road toward the few hundred men of Task Force Smith were thirty-three T-34 tanks and about ten thousand North Korean soldiers. The U.S. howitzers fired on the tanks and hit them, but those mighty tanks simply kept moving. The task force howitzer teams couldn't make a dent. Mud and enemy fire were everywhere. Finally, Smith ordered his men to retreat toward Pusan. Many threw away their heavy weapons. They even left behind their dead and wounded. The task force lost about one-third of its men that day.

The North Korean army continued its advance toward Pusan. Again, the United States asked the UN to help. And again the UN was able to act because the Soviet delegate was absent from the Security Council. This time the council resolved that "the members of the United Nations furnish such assistance . . . [to South Korea] as may be necessary to repel the armed attacks and to restore international peace and security to the area."

A U.S. gun crew fires a howitzer to halt advancing North Koreans.

Twenty-one members of the United Nations, including the United States, agreed to defend South Korea. Some nations contributed troops. Others gave nonmilitary aid, such as ambulances and hospital ships. The UN asked President Truman to appoint a military leader. As expected, Truman named General MacArthur supreme commander of UN forces. MacArthur asked for more troops and better equipment. He got both.

FIGHTING FOR TIME

Major General William Dean arrived at Pusan with U.S. soldiers of the Twenty-fourth Infantry Regiment. They met the retreating Task Force Smith and tried to dig in behind the Kum River, just north of the city of Taejon. But their lines crumbled against the North Koreans.

The War That Wasn't

The president of the United States is also commander in chief of U.S. military forces. So, as commander in chief, Truman could order U.S. troops into combat. But he could not declare war because the power to do that lies with Congress. President Truman did not request a formal declaration of war from Congress. He knew that the North Korean army might take over South Korea in less time than it would take for Congress to debate a declaration of war.

Meeting with reporters, Truman said, "We are not at war." But when a reporter asked if this was a "police action," Truman nodded yes. From then on, the war in Korea was often referred to as a police action.

MINORITIES IN THE KOREAN WAR

In 1948 President Truman issued Executive Order 9981. It required "equality of treatment and opportunity for all persons in the armed services without regard to race, color, religion, or national origin." Previously, the armed forces had been strictly segregated. Blacks served in separate units. Despite the new order, integration came slowly for African American soldiers.

In 1950 about ten percent of soldiers in the U.S. Army were black. Most of them were in service and supply units, rather than combat units. One exception was the all-black Twenty-fourth Infantry Regiment. The regiment proudly traced its roots to the Buffalo Soldiers—the all-black unit that fought in the American West in the late 1800s.

The African American Twenty-fourth Infantry was one of the first groups to be sent to Korea. President Truman had banned segregation in the army some years earlier, but integration of the troops came slowly.

The four thousand men of the Twenty-fourth Infantry were stationed in Japan after World War II. Like many other U.S. soldiers there, they enjoyed the pleasures of a peacetime army and were poorly prepared for combat in Korea. When war came, however, the Twenty-fourth Infantry was one of the first U.S. groups to go to Korea. With them went three other all-black units, as well as two companies of white soldiers.

William Thompson, a member of the Twenty-fourth Infantry Regiment, earned the war's first Medal of Honor—the military's highest award. Private First Class Thompson was also the first African American to receive the Medal of Honor since 1898. As part of the Army's move toward integration, the Twenty-fourth was eventually disbanded.

Meanwhile, the National Association for the Advancement of Colored People (NAACP) received many letters from soldiers in Korea. They described how African American soldiers suffered under segregation, were unfairly convicted of crimes, and were given more severe sentences than white soldiers.

Thurgood Marshall—the NAACP's chief lawyer—went to Japan and Korea in January 1951 with President Truman's permission. Marshall visited black troops on the front lines in Korea and investigated the cases of thirty-six African American soldiers in prison in Japan. He was able to reduce the sentences for most of these soldiers.

The U.S. Air Force was less segregated than the army. Daniel "Chappie" James Jr. became the first black commander of an integrated air force squadron. James flew P-51 Mustang fighter planes, then switched to jet fighters. After completing one hundred combat missions, he went to the Philippines to train pilots for combat in Korea. James later became America's first black four-star general.

Most other minorities were integrated into military units in the Korean War. One exception was the Sixty-fifth Infantry Regiment, which came from Puerto Rico. They stayed together throughout the war, often fighting on the front lines. The regiment called itself "The Borinqueneers," from the Arawak Indian name for Puerto Rico.

John Rice, a Native American soldier, was killed in Korea. When his body was sent home to Sioux City, Iowa, officials of the cemetery there refused to bury him because he "was not a member of the Caucasian race." President Truman sent an air force plane to bring Rice and his family to Washington, D.C. Truman arranged for Sergeant Rice to be buried at Arlington National Cemetery with full military honors.

The Puerto Rican Borinqueneers fought together in the Korean War.

South Korean soldiers joined U.S. soldiers in an attempt to hold the area around Taejon.

On July 19, the North Korean army attacked Taejon and burned the city. The Twenty-fourth Infantry Regiment was forced to retreat, and the North Koreans captured General Dean. After only two weeks in battle, only half of the sixteen thousand men in the Twenty-fourth Infantry Regiment were still able to fight. More than twenty-four hundred men were dead or missing in action.

On July 29, General Walton Walker met troop commanders at Sangju, about forty miles east of Taejon. "We are fighting a battle against time," he said. "There will be no more retreating. . . . There is no line behind us to which we can retreat . . . [and] a retreat to Pusan would be one of the greatest butcheries in history. . . . We are going

Who Is the Enemy?

During the chaos that followed the first few weeks of the war, a company of U.S. soldiers killed more than one hundred unarmed civilians in the South Korean village of No Gun Ri. Survivors later asked the governments of South Korea and the United States to apologize and to pay compensation. In 2001 President Bill Clinton offered an expression of deep regret for what had happened at No Gun Ri but without acknowledging any U.S. wrongdoing.

to hold the line. We are going to win."

Soviet tanks were not the only reason for North Korean victories. U.S. forces were up against a well-trained enemy. Many soldiers in the North Korean army had fought with

Two women, South Korean fighters, are in charge of a machine gun to help hold back the North Korean push into South Korea.

U.S. Marines move through a rice paddy.

the Chinese Communists against the Japanese army in World War II and against the Chinese Nationalists afterward. They were disciplined and determined.

The North Koreans were fighting on territory that was familiar to them. They could range through the countryside and often attacked at night. Small groups of soldiers sneaked behind U.S. positions. When U.S. forces were attacked and began to retreat, they would run into enemy soldiers on all sides. It made them think they were surrounded. North Korean soldiers engaged in closer combat than U.S. soldiers were used to, firing their weapons at close range. This kind of combat made it difficult for U.S. planes to attack the North Koreans on the ground without killing their own soldiers.

The summer of 1950 was one of the hottest in years in Korea. Temperatures soared to over one hundred degrees Fahrenheit. Heavy rains brought little relief and a lot of mud. Desperately hot and thirsty, U.S. soldiers, unused to the weather, often scooped up water from rice paddies (flooded fields where rice is grown). If they didn't use water purification tablets, these soldiers were likely to get sick with diarrhea and dysentery.

Fresh troops from the United States and other UN nations continued to arrive in Pusan. They headed for the front lines in a brave attempt to stop the invasion. General MacArthur, in charge of all UN troops, described a bold strategy for winning the war. Nearly everyone thought it was crazy. These were desperate times, however. President Truman gave MacArthur permission to proceed with this plan. But the earliest time it could be carried out was the middle of September, weeks away, and it wasn't certain that UN forces could hold out that long.

EYEWITNESS QUOTE:

"The July heat was intense and the flies swarming about were green, large and heavy."

—Captain Oree Gregory, a nurse in South Korea

SAVING
3) THE SOUTH

Every hour that U.S. and South Korean troops could delay the North Korean push southward, the more troops and supplies could be landed at Pusan, on the southeast tip of Korea. The UN forces gathering there were called the Eighth Army, and they were commanded by Walton Walker, a U.S. lieutenant general. Walker's Eighth Army formed a 140-mile defensive ring around the city, called the Pusan Perimeter.

Kim Il Sung, the leader of North Korea, wanted to capture Pusan by August 15, 1950. This date marked the fifth anniversary of Liberation Day (when Japan gave up control of Korea). But by early August, U.S. and UN warships completely controlled the sea lanes around Pusan. U.S. planes controlled the skies above it. This made it possible for fresh troops to land every day.

Soon about ninety-two thousand UN troops (including the South Koreans) were defending Pusan from inside the perimeter. This included a group of thirty thousand to forty thousand people known as the Korean Augmentation of the US Army or KATUSA. This group was mostly made up of school-aged boys living on the streets of Pusan and the city of Taegu, just outside the perimeter. They assisted U.S. forces with a variety of jobs, such as scouting out enemy troop movements, guarding prisoners of war (POWs), and helping Korean refugees.

Some seventy thousand soldiers of the North Korean army, along with their tanks, airplanes, and heavy artillery, were sent to break the Pusan Perimeter. But the closer the North Korean army got to Pusan, the longer their supply lines were. These long supply lines made it harder to maintain a fresh, well-equipped fighting force. UN forces were able to bring in fresh supplies from Japan, and they had good supply lines in and around Pusan. Their soldiers were well fed and could receive prompt and expert medical care.

The North Korean army struck in a series of attacks, but UN soldiers managed

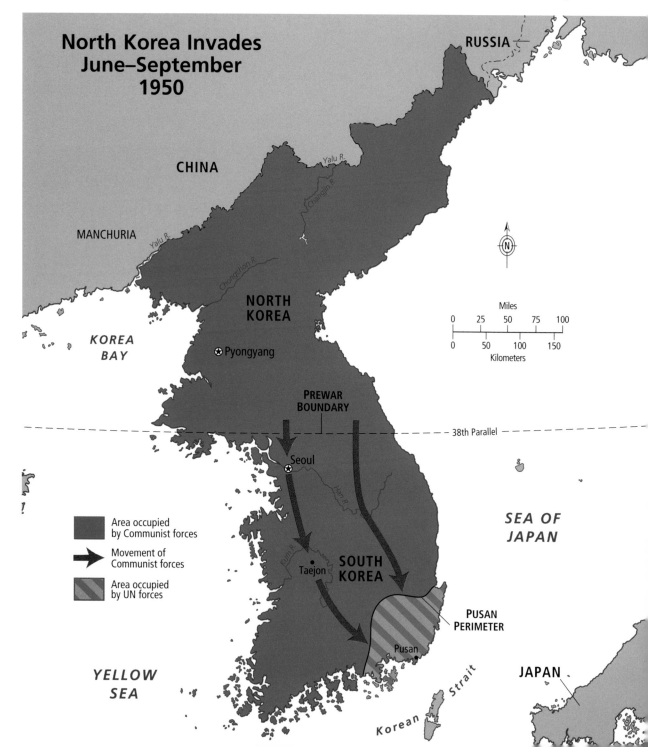

North Korea Invades June–September 1950

RUSSIA

CHINA

Yalu R.

Changjin R.

MANCHURIA

Yalu R.

Chongchon R.

NORTH KOREA

KOREA BAY

⊗ Pyongyang

Miles
0   25   50   75   100

0   50   100   150
Kilometers

PREWAR BOUNDARY

— 38th Parallel —

⊗ Seoul

Han R.

SEA OF JAPAN

Kum R.

Taejon •

SOUTH KOREA

Area occupied by Communist forces

Movement of Communist forces

Area occupied by UN forces

PUSAN PERIMETER

Pusan •

YELLOW SEA

Korean Strait

JAPAN

Two hundred and fifty ships with heavy air support were involved in Operation **CHROMITE**.

to defend themselves. UN airplanes dropped bombs and napalm on the advancing North Korean troops. Intelligence officers broke enemy codes and learned where the North Koreans planned to strike next. General Walker directed Eighth Army forces to head off the attack.

FAST FACT

NAPALM

Napalm is a jellied form of gasoline used in bombs and other explosive devices. When these explode, the burning jelly flies out. It clings to objects and people and sets them on fire.

August came and went without the victory Kim wanted. The North Korean army launched a general offensive all along the Pusan Perimeter in the hope that the UN's defensive line might break somewhere. But the perimeter held and was even beginning to expand. By September 10, UN forces had recaptured Taegu, some sixty miles north of Pusan. Fighting was fierce. More U.S. soldiers died in the first fifteen days of September 1950 than in any other fifteen-day period of the Korean War.

INCHON SURPRISE

Just when the Eighth Army along the Pusan Perimeter was getting strong enough to push the North Koreans back toward the 38th Parallel, General MacArthur decided to open a second front behind enemy lines. He launched Operation CHROMITE. With more than seventy thousand troops, some 250 ships and transport vehicles, and heavy air support, Operation CHROMITE was one of the strongest offensives in the Korean War.

General MacArthur planned to trap the North Korean army between two UN forces and to cut off their supply lines. He established the X (Tenth) Corps under Major General Edward Almond. Then he announced that the X Corps was going to attack Inchon, a port city on the west coast about twenty miles from Seoul.

Inchon was deep within territory held by the North Koreans. The actual harbor was about ten miles inland from the Yellow Sea. Between the harbor and the sea was a narrow, winding channel of water with huge mud flats on either side. Tides varied widely hour by hour, and there were only three days left in 1950 when the water in the channel would be deep enough for landing ships to make it into the harbor. September 15 was the next time the tide would be high enough, according to one tide chart.

As if the tricky channel and difficult tides weren't problem enough, the harbor was protected by fortifications and heavy artillery on Wolmi-do (Moon Tip Island). Several hills on the mainland also dominated the harbor. And it was possible that the harbor had been mined to blow up any ships trying to land at Inchon.

The Joint Chiefs of Staff reminded General MacArthur of how difficult it would be to take Inchon, but MacArthur was confident. MacArthur responded, "The very arguments you have made . . . will tend to ensure for me the element of surprise. For the North Korean commander will reason that no one would be so brash as to make such an attempt. . . . We must act now or we will die. . . . We shall land at Inchon and I shall crush them."

Nations United

Fifteen other nations besides South Korea and the United States sent troops to fight in the Korean War. They were Australia, Belgium, Canada, Colombia, Ethiopia, France, Great Britain, Greece, Luxembourg, the Netherlands, New Zealand, the Philippines, Thailand, Turkey, and South Africa. Some nations sent thousands of people, others only a few. The United States sent more than five million men and women to the Korean War—more troops than all the other UN members and South Korea combined.

Five members of the UN decided to provide aid to South Korea rather than troops. Denmark supplied a hospital ship. Sweden, Norway, and Italy each supplied field hospitals. And India, which had just gained independence from Great Britain in 1947, contributed an ambulance.

To keep the enemy from learning their true target, UN forces staged naval and air attacks at several port cities. They included Inchon and Kunsan, about one hundred miles south of Inchon. Marine officers in Pusan spoke loudly to their troops about the landing beaches at Kunsan, in case spies were nearby. Not everyone was fooled. China's leader, Mao Zedong, warned Stalin and Kim Il Sung that the UN might strike at Inchon. But they ignored him.

On September 15, the tide was high enough for UN warships to sail up the channel toward Inchon. Airplanes flew ahead of the warships, raining down machine-gun fire on the North Korean soldiers occupying the island fortress of Wolmi-do. At 6:33 A.M., the first marines charged onto the island (called "Green Beach" in their battle plans). At 6:55 A.M., Sergeant Alvin Smith tied a U.S. flag to the top of a half-burned tree on the island. General MacArthur, who was watching from the bridge of the warship *Mount McKinley,* saw the flag and said, "That's it. Let's get a cup of coffee."

For the UN troops on Wolmi-do, there was more to do than have a cup of coffee. With the aid of tanks, flamethrowers, and other weapons, they killed or captured enemy soldiers. They used a Sherman tank with a bulldozer blade to bury alive a group of North Korean soldiers in a foxhole. By about 8:00 A.M., Wolmi-do was in the hands of the marines. Then, as the tide went out, they were completely stranded on the island, surrounded by a sea of mud.

When the tide was again high enough hours later, troops began the assault on Red Beach, an area of Inchon northeast of Wolmi-do, and on Blue Beach, about three miles south of Red Beach. The attack force launched thousands of rockets ashore, causing great clouds of dust and smoke. Amtracs (amphibious tractors, which could run on both water and land) brought in the troops. They raced toward a fifteen-foot high seawall that protected the city. The seawall at Blue Beach was broken in many places, and the troops and amtracs scrambled through. On Red Beach, troops used wooden ladders and climbed over the seawall. With them came three reporters, including Marguerite Higgins, who was carrying her typewriter.

The forces on Wolmi-do met up with those on Red Beach. By the next morn-

Douglas MacArthur, (seated, center) on the warship *Mount McKinley*, supervised the shelling of Inchon Harbor.

LSTs (landing ship tanks) unload men and equipment on a beach at Inchon.

ing, the Red Beach and Blue Beach forces had overrun Inchon and met on the south side of the city. They encountered some gunfire but relatively little resistance. Air and naval bombardments had destroyed much of the city. But Inchon had been taken back from the North Koreans. With enemy forces retreating in front of them, UN troops moved on to recapture Seoul.

Devotion to Duty

First Lieutenant Baldomero Lopez led his platoon of marines climbing over the seawall at Inchon on September 15, 1950. Moments later, Lopez moved toward an enemy bunker and got out a hand grenade. As he pulled the grenade pin, Lopez was shot in the right shoulder and chest. He fell backward and dropped the grenade near his own platoon. Lopez crawled over to this mini-time bomb but realized he no longer had the strength to hurl it into the enemy bunker. He forced the grenade under his body and smothered the explosion. Lopez killed himself to save his men.

Marines climb onto the seawall at Inchon.

WOMEN IN THE KOREAN WAR

In 1950 about twenty-two thousand women were in the U.S. armed services. These included members of the Women's Army Corps (WAC), Women in the Air Force (WAF), Women Accepted for Volunteer Emergency Service (Navy WAVES), and Women Marines. About one-third of these women were in the medical field. The rest had noncombat assignments. They put parachutes in condition to use, coded and decoded messages, operated military radios, and did many other jobs. When off duty, they sent stationery, food, and books to soldiers in "adopted" combat units and knitted them woolen socks and sweaters. They also gave blood.

An army nurse explains how wounded soldiers should be loaded into a plane to take them to a military hospital.

In 1951 about two hundred WACs were called from reserve status into active duty. This was the first time U.S. women were ever called to serve without their consent.

Army nurses stationed in Japan went to Korea four days after the first U.S. troops arrived there. They set up a hospital in Pusan and two days later moved with a Mobile Army Surgical Hospital (MASH) to the front lines.

Army Nurse Corps women (men could not join then) worked in temporary field hospitals, regular hospitals, MASH units, and on hospital trains. They often lived under the same conditions as soldiers and worked with nurses from other UN countries. Air Force nurses cared for wounded soldiers being flown to hospitals in Japan. Navy nurses served on hospital ships, which might move as the front lines changed. Although U.S. nurses could transfer to hospitals in Japan after three months in Korea, most chose to stay.

Thousands of military and civilian women showed bravery and endured hardship during the Korean War. One example is Viola McConnel, the only U.S. army nurse on duty in Korea when North Korea attacked. Captain McConnel crammed 682 people—mostly non-Korean civilians—into a Norwegian freighter normally carrying twelve passengers. During the perilous two-day trip from Korea to Japan, she went without sleep to care for them—including an adult with a fractured skull and a baby with pneumonia.

Newspaper reporter Marguerite Higgins fought to be allowed to enter combat zones.

American Red Cross volunteers sent to Korea included about forty women who worked in canteens, or clubs, primarily providing food and recreation to UN forces, though Red Cross regulations prohibited them from dancing with the soldiers. Other women, known as Gray Ladies, served as volunteers in military hospitals in the United States and Japan.

The best-known U.S. woman in the Korean War was Marguerite Higgins, a reporter for the *New York Herald*. General Walker wanted to ban her from entering combat zones, but she fought to stay.

"I felt that my position as a correspondent was at stake," she said. "I could not let the fact that I was a woman jeopardize my newspaper's coverage of the war." Higgins spent most of the war on the front lines. She said, "If you worried about being shot at, you'd never get a story." One soldier described Higgins as "the bravest woman I ever knew."

Less than one percent of the U.S. citizens serving in Korea during the war were women. Some Korean women also served in the South Korean army in a group called the Korean Women's Army. Women served in the North Korean army as well.

Members of the Korean Women's Army wore white headbands as part of their uniform.

RECAPTURING SEOUL AND MOVING ON

For much of the way from Inchon to Seoul, UN troops traveled in their massive amtracs, protected by M26 tanks. The fighting became fiercer as they neared the city. By September 17, UN troops reached Kimpo Airfield, about eight miles from Seoul. Kimpo was the most important airfield in Korea. The North Korean troops waged a series of attacks in an effort to keep Kimpo, but the UN defeated them. Soon U.S. Corsair bombers, using Kimpo, were giving UN forces the air power they needed to retake Seoul.

The battle for Seoul was nothing like the battle for Inchon. The North Korean army dug in and attacked again and again with deadly force. Finally, after a week of fighting in barricaded streets and burning buildings, the UN's X Corps claimed victory.

On September 29, MacArthur met South Korea's president, Syngman Rhee, at Kimpo Airfield. The two men, their escorts, and the reporters who often followed MacArthur drove through the nearly destroyed capital to the battered National Assembly building. MacArthur returned Seoul to Rhee with these words:

UN soldiers faced fierce, close fighting in the streets of Seoul.

Two boys, members of the North Korean army, are questioned by a U.S. soldier after their capture.

"On behalf of the United Nations Command, I am happy to restore to you, Mr. President, the seat of your government, that from it you may better fulfill your constitutional responsibilities."

By the time X Corps had given Seoul back to Syngman Rhee, the Eighth Army had broken through North Korean forces attacking the Pusan Perimeter and was speeding northward. Caught between these two UN forces, the North Korean army broke into thousands of small groups, each trying to retreat across the 38th Parallel. Under unending attack by aircraft and ground troops, many North Korean soldiers were killed or captured. Of the seventy thousand or so North Koreans who had chased UN forces south to Pusan, roughly twenty-five thousand to thirty thousand managed to return to North Korea using mountain passes and back roads.

Kim Il Sung had invaded South Korea on June 25, 1950, in hopes of reuniting Korea under Communist rule by August 15. By the end of September, it seemed the only North Korean soldiers left south of the 38th Parallel were prisoners.

> **EYEWITNESS QUOTE: CAPTURE OF SEOUL**
>
> "All I know about a fleeing enemy is that there's two or three hundred out there that won't be fleeing anymore. They're dead."
>
> —Colonel Lewis Puller

NORTH TO
4 THE YALU–ALMOST

When war started, the United Nations agreed only to prevent the North Korean army from taking Korea south of the 38th Parallel. The UN commander General MacArthur and South Korean president Rhee wanted to continue north to topple the North Korean government and establish a united Korea. President Truman and the Joint Chiefs of Staff agreed with this plan. Speaking about the 38th Parallel, Secretary of State Acheson said, "Troops could not be expected . . . to march up to a surveyor's line and stop."

MacArthur was authorized to destroy the North Korean army. UN troops would be allowed to cross the 38th only if there was no sign that China or the Soviet Union would get involved in the war.

On October 1, South Korean soldiers surged across the 38th Parallel into North Korea. MacArthur called for North Korea's leader, Kim Il Sung, to surrender. Kim did no such thing. Instead, China warned the United States that Chinese troops would aid Kim if U.S. or UN troops crossed into North Korea. The Chinese also said that they would not take action if only South Korean troops crossed the border. The Chinese Nationalists in Taiwan also warned that the Chinese Communists would aid the North Koreans if U.S. troops entered North Korea. The main U.S. spy organization, the Central Intelligence Agency (CIA),

I'm with You

As UN forces raced toward Pyongyang, the North Korean capital, in October 1950, North Korean soldiers fled the city in droves. Enemy troops often crossed each other's lines. An Australian officer from the UN found himself in the midst of North Korean troops. He walked through them mumbling, "Rusky, Rusky" ("Russian, Russian"). Thinking he was a Russian adviser from the Soviet Union, the North Koreans not only let him pass but gave him a few pats on the back.

on the other hand, reported that China was not eager to fight. No one was sure about the Soviet Union.

About a week after South Korean troops entered North Korea, the UN decided that "all appropriate steps be taken to ensure conditions of stability throughout Korea." U.S. troops then crossed into North Korea. In order to show that the United States didn't intend to attack China, the Joint Chiefs directed MacArthur to get authorization from Washington before striking Chinese territory.

On October 9, MacArthur again proposed that Kim surrender. The Soviet delegate to the UN proposed that all foreign troops leave Korea. Both proposals were ignored, and the fighting continued.

President Truman decided to meet with MacArthur to discuss the situation. They met on Wake Island, a tiny piece of land in the Pacific Ocean. Truman flew more than fourteen thousand miles round trip. He had a one-hour private meeting with the general and another ninety-minute conference with MacArthur and military and political advisers.

MacArthur advised Truman that even if China entered the war, only about fifty thousand Chinese soldiers might get across the Yalu River, which separated China and North Korea. MacArthur assured Truman that any Chinese invaders would be soundly defeated. U.S. troops would be home by Christmas 1950. Truman left Wake Island satisfied. As

President Truman and General MacArthur met on tiny Wake Island in the Pacific Ocean.

MacArthur prepared to leave, he invited reporters to come to Pyongyang, the capital of North Korea. "It won't be long now," he said.

MacArthur then decided to divide the UN forces in two. The Eighth Army under General Walker would cover the western half of North Korea, crossing north from the 38th Parallel. The X Corps under General Almond would land at the port of Wonsan on the east coast about one hundred miles north of the 38th. Just as Inchon was the "left hook" that knocked out the North Korean army in the South, Wonsan would be the "right hook" that would help the UN conquer North Korea. The two UN forces would operate with little radio contact and a lot of mountainous ter-

> **EYEWITNESS QUOTE:**
> **CHINA TO THE RESCUE**
>
> "After hesitation and a series of provisional decisions, the Chinese comrades at last [have] made a final decision to render assistance to Korea with troops."
>
> —A cable to Kim Il Sung from Mao Zedong, October 13, 1950

rain between them. The plan was for the Eighth Army and X Corps to independently drive enemy troops to the Yalu River on the northern border of Korea. Then Kim Il Sung would finally surrender. It didn't happen that way.

CHINA GOES TO WAR

No one at the Wake Island conference knew that the day before the conference Mao had told Stalin that China would help North Korea. Chinese soldiers serving in Manchuria as the Northeast Border Defense Force became the Chinese People's Volunteers. But there was nothing voluntary about them. They were troops from the regular Chinese army.

At least three hundred thousand Chinese soldiers began to move toward the

Miserable Marines Miss Marilyn

The marines who sailed to Wonsan on North Korea's east coast were supposed to be the first UN forces there. Instead, they were delayed for weeks at sea as minesweepers cleared mines around Wonsan harbor. Overcrowding, high seas, and low provisions resulted in what one marine called an "ordeal of misery and sickness." Meanwhile, land forces took the city. It seemed everybody got to Wonsan before the floating marines, including a show that entertained UN troops. The marines even missed seeing the glamorous movie star Marilyn Monroe (at right in Korea)!

Skyraiders and other attack planes fired on North Korean forces as they fled Pyongyang.

northern banks of the Yalu River. They were commanded by Peng Dehai, an experienced and highly capable military leader. To keep their movements a secret, they lit no fires, marched mostly at night, and hid in the forest-covered mountains during the day. They carried their own rations (mostly cooked rice and beans) and weapons in one-hundred-pound bundles on their backs. This army had few trucks or pieces of heavy equipment, and the soldiers brushed away any tracks their tires made in the snow. UN pilots patrolling along the Yalu River had no idea so many Chinese soldiers were massing along the border.

General Peng and Kim Il Sung mapped out their strategy. The Chinese troops would be joined by the remaining North Korean soldiers, an estimated forty thousand to sixty thousand troops. Part of the combined forces would challenge the

Eighth Army in the western part of North Korea. The other part would attack X Corps in eastern North Korea. They planned to allow UN troops to advance deep into cold, mountainous territory, harassed only by North Korean soldiers. The Chinese would attack after UN communication and supply lines were stretched out and weakened.

Of course, General MacArthur did not know about the plans Peng and Kim had made. UN units raced to be the first to capture Pyongyang. The North Korean army was under heavy fire from UN airplanes. The North Koreans had left most of their tanks and large weapons in South Korea and were unable to mount a strong defense. Thousands of North Korean soldiers surrendered or fled in disarray.

On October 19, Pyongyang fell to the Eighth Army. Kim and his government officials set up temporary headquarters at Sinuiju on the Yalu River. UN

EYEWITNESS QUOTE:
PENG'S PLAN

"We will employ a strategy of luring the enemy forces into our internal line and wiping them out one by one."

—Chinese commander Peng Dehai

"I Had Two"

The great U.S. actor and singer Al Jolson *(right)* flew to Pyongyang to entertain UN troops after they captured that city on October 19, 1950. Jolson, 62, entertained U.S. troops so often they called him "G. I. Jolson." Back in San Francisco, California, on October 23, Jolson suffered a fatal heart attack. Shortly before he died, Jolson is said to have joked, "You know, President Truman only had one hour with General MacArthur. I had two."

forces continued northward the next day, advancing to the Chongchon River. The Yalu River was only about sixty miles farther north. Meanwhile, X Corps troops on the east coast of Korea had captured Wonsan and were also moving northward.

TOO FAR AND TOO COLD

MacArthur was sure victory was just around the corner. On October 24, he ordered all UN troops to speed toward the Yalu River. The Joint Chiefs of Staff were furious. They had told MacArthur that only South Korean troops should push to the Yalu River. President Truman wanted to make it clear to the Chinese and the Soviets that the United States did not wish to attack their countries. MacArthur, they decided, had literally gone too far.

On October 25, a large number of Chinese soldiers attacked UN forces. A South Korean regiment near Unsan, close to the Yalu River, was fired on. South Korean General Paik Sun Yup reported that even though the three hundred or so enemy troops there wore North Korean uniforms, at least some of them were Chinese. A prisoner captured by Paik's men could not speak Korean but was fluent in Chinese. He spoke of many other Chinese soldiers in the area.

Other South Korean soldiers were attacked near Onjong. Lieutenant Glen Jones, their U.S. military adviser, was with them. When Jones was captured, the Chinese had proof that U.S. troops were fighting far north of the 38th Parallel. Jones later died in a POW camp.

Over the next week, Chinese and North Korean attacks increased dramatically against the Eighth Army and X Corps. November 1 brought two surprises to U.S. forces—both bad. Until then, UN planes completely dominated the airspace over Korea. But on November 1, several UN planes on a mission close to the Yalu River were suddenly attacked by six jet fighters. These MiG-15s were the latest and deadliest Soviet aircraft. U.S. pilots had never seen them before. The UN planes took evasive action and returned to base safely.

A battalion of U.S. troops near Unsan was not as lucky that day. Just after dusk, Chinese forces staged a ferocious attack.

Help-Icopter

Captain George Farish was flying his VMO-6 helicopter on a spy mission over North Korea when he noticed that dried rice plants had been arranged in an open field to spell "HELP." As soon as Farish warily landed in the field, Private First Class William Meister, who had been missing in action, came out of hiding and hitched a ride to safety.

Relief forces later came upon an eerie scene of about six hundred frozen corpses. Not one U.S. soldier had survived.

Like the North Korean army, the Chinese People's Volunteers often attacked at night and tried to surround the UN forces. Only one in five Chinese soldiers carried a rifle, and many of their weapons had been taken from Japanese troops in China during World War II. But hand grenades were plentiful, and the Chinese People's Volunteers had combat experience fighting the Japanese and the Nationalist Chinese. They were familiar with the terrain and weather conditions in the northern part of Korea.

During an attack, Chinese troops shouted loudly, blew whistles, and beat drums and gongs. These noises were simply an easy way to communicate among the scattered, poorly equipped Chinese units. But the noises during a nighttime attack frightened and confused UN troops.

In the heavy combat that followed November 1, more UN troops were sent to the front lines. Chinese and North Korean troops killed or captured many UN soldiers before the UN units pulled back. In the eastern part of North Korea, however, marines had the upper hand for a few days. In combined air and ground strikes, they killed hundreds of Chinese soldiers near the Chosin Reservoir.

U. S. Marines capture Chinese Communist soldiers in central Korea.

A Russian-built MiG-15 is shot down over North Korea

On November 8, the MiG-15 jets struck again, this time against a group of B-29 bombers and F-80 jet fighters. This was the first jet-to-jet air battle in history. F-80 pilot Lieutenant Russell Brown shot down one of the MiGs. The remaining fighters abandoned their attack. Neither the United States nor the Soviet Union revealed that the pilot of the downed jet fighter was a Soviet airman. Neither country wanted to expand the war in Korea into a battle between two nations that had atomic bombs.

By November the winter in the north was cruelly cold. Despite the weather, General MacArthur ordered UN forces to press on toward the Yalu River. Without first asking the Joint Chiefs of Staff, he ordered UN pilots to blow up the twelve main bridges over the Yalu that linked Chinese Manchuria with North Korea. MacArthur argued that destroying the bridges was necessary from a military point of view. But he ignored the political aspect of the act. Chinese leaders might see the bombing of these bridges into their country as an act of war against China and send even more Chinese troops into Korea.

The Joint Chiefs struck a strange compromise. They allowed MacArthur to bomb only the North Korean half of the bridges, destroying them to their midpoint. And they ordered MacArthur not to destroy the Yalu's hydroelectric plants, which supplied power to China and part of the Soviet Union.

U.S. Marines sit covered with snow and ice near the Chosin Reservoir.

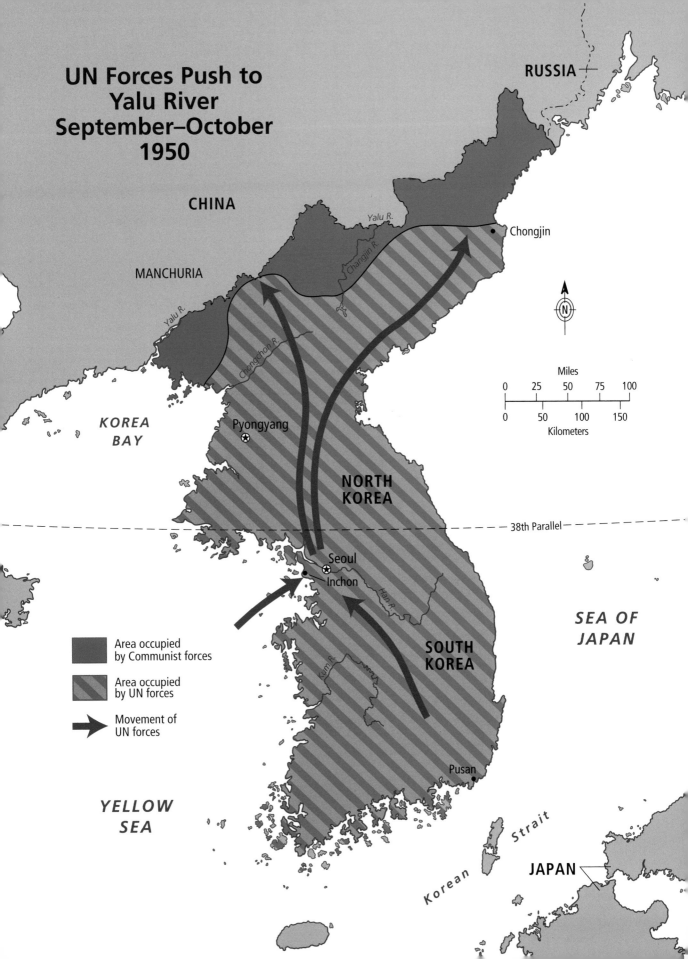

UN Forces Push to Yalu River September–October 1950

RUSSIA

CHINA

MANCHURIA

Yalu R.

Changjin R.

Chongjin

Yalu R.

Chongchon R.

KOREA BAY

Pyongyang ✪

NORTH KOREA

Miles
0   25   50   75   100
0   50   100   150
Kilometers

38th Parallel

Seoul ✪
Inchon
Han R.

SEA OF JAPAN

Kum R.

SOUTH KOREA

Area occupied by Communist forces

Area occupied by UN forces

Movement of UN forces

Pusan

YELLOW SEA

Korean Strait

JAPAN

Navy bombers drop bombs on the Korean side of bridges over the Yalu River.

Only a few weeks earlier on Wake Island, MacArthur had assured President Truman that the few troops China might put in Korea would be easily defeated. This time MacArthur argued that Chinese forces could overwhelm the UN forces. Even the North Korean troops were a continuing threat. But as U.S. military leaders discussed these problems, something odd happened on the battlefield. After November 6, Chinese soldiers pulled back into the frozen mountains and stopped fighting.

Some of the president's advisers thought that the Chinese People's Volunteers were waiting for better weather to launch another offensive. Other advisers thought China was giving the UN a chance to reconsider its military aims. No one knew for sure. General MacArthur ordered his troops to rest, but he still planned to conquer all of North Korea. He planned to resume his home-by-Christmas offensive by Thanksgiving Day.

Happy Birthday!

On November 10, 1950, soldiers of the First Marine Division decided to celebrate the 175th birthday of the U.S. Marine Corps—no matter that they were hunkered down at Majon-ni deep inside North Korea. The marines invited their South Korean allies to join in what was described as a "brief but heartfelt celebration [featuring an] ambitiously large cake smeared with C-Ration jam."

THE ENEMY'S POINT OF VIEW

When the Communists took power in North Korea, they portrayed the United States as an imperial (dominating) power determined to spread the evils of capitalism to Asia. Koreans had been told the same thing during the Japanese occupation of their country. Chung Dong-kyu remembers that at school, "I had been instructed by my Japanese masters to hate the American and British imperialists. In fact, every morning I spent in school during World War II, I had jabbed my wooden bayonet into straw dummies whose faces were the caricatures of Franklin Roosevelt's and Winston Churchill's." (Winston Churchill was prime minister of Great Britain at the time.)

Waves of North Korean refugees flooded South Korea, seeking better economic and political conditions there. Chung was among them—he later came to the United States, changed his name to Donald K. Chung, and became a heart surgeon. However, Kim Il Sung and his government continued to portray the United States as an enemy of an independent Korea.

The Communist Chinese, under Mao Zedong, also portrayed the United States as a power-hungry nation, no different from the Japanese who had occupied Korea and China. The *People's Daily* (a government-controlled newspaper) put it this way: "We Chinese people are against the American imperialists because they are against us."

Thousands of North Koreans fled from the Chinese troops gathering in Pyongyang in 1950.

In November 1950, General MacArthur commanded UN troops to invade all of North Korea. As U.S. forces approached the Chinese border at the Yalu River, Chinese General Peng commented on U.S. actions: "The U.S. occupation of Korea, separated from China only by a river, would threaten northeast China. . . . If the United States wanted to invade China, we had to stop its aggressions. Without a test with U.S. imperialism to see who was stronger, it would be difficult for us to build socialism."

China's people were exhausted from years of civil war and war against Japan. So the Chinese government tried to boost their morale for fighting in Korea. Soldiers' families had preference in receiving food, scarce consumer goods, and jobs. There were even special shops for these "Glorious Families." But over time, the heavy loss of Chinese troops dampened enthusiasm for the war.

"AN ENTIRELY
5 NEW WAR"

Determined to force North Korea to surrender, General MacArthur ordered his troops to march toward the Yalu River on November 24, 1950, the day after Thanksgiving. This win-the-war offensive came just as cold weather tore into the troops. Temperatures at night fell to around twenty degrees below zero Fahrenheit. Winds often rose to thirty miles per hour. Weapons froze, medicines froze, and people's body parts froze. Hundreds of soldiers suffered from frostbite or collapsed from the cold.

The Eighth Army crossed the Chongchon River and headed north on icy roads. Suddenly some 180,000 Chinese troops poured down the snowy hillsides and rained mortar and rifle fire on UN troops. The Chinese People's Volunteers took thousands of prisoners, who were promised peace and safety if they surrendered. Many of these prisoners froze to death as they marched to prison camps.

Air attacks by UN forces could not stop the Chinese onslaught. But they did kill Mao Anyang, the oldest son of Mao Zedong, when they dropped napalm on his army unit. Mao Anyang was a staff officer for General Peng.

On November 24, the X Corps in the eastern part of North Korea also began its win-the-war offensive. Five days earlier, they had started to hack out an airfield from a frozen bean field at Hagaru, about twelve miles south of the Chosin Reservoir. It took the soldiers only twelve days to make a suitable landing strip. The airfield was supposed to be used to support air attacks in North Korea. But when Chinese forces attacked the X Corps, the Hagaru airfield became a vital way to evacuate wounded soldiers. C-47 cargo planes took more than four thousand patients to safety before the UN troops were forced to retreat.

Between UN air attacks and Chinese ground attacks, both sides suffered many casualties, dead and wounded. Still the Chinese kept pushing forward. By the end of November, most of the UN forces were being pushed back toward South Korea. The Eighth Army pulled back toward Seoul, while most of the X Corps made for the east coast ports of Hungnam and Wonsan. About twenty thousand marines in the X Corps remained trapped in several positions by about one hundred thousand enemy soldiers. Their most northern position—at Yudam-ni—was more than seventy-five miles from the coast, along an icy, narrow dirt road. Their situation seemed hopeless.

On December 1, these marines began their push to the sea. Their commander, Major General Oliver Smith, never spoke of retreat. Instead, he said the marines were "attacking in another direction."

With UN air strikes covering them, Smith's marines fought their way south through the mountains near the Chosin Reservoir in deadly cold and dense fog. Civilians fleeing the fighting clogged the roads. The marines inched their way down to Hagaru, then to Koto-ri. And there, under deadly fire, they had to stop. The marines knew that Chinese forces had blown up the bridge spanning the chasm (deep valley) at Funchilin Pass, just south of Koto-ri. There was no way to go around the chasm, and even marines couldn't march across twenty-four feet of thin air.

Losing Faith

In the mountains of North Korea, it was so cold that soldiers had to urinate on their rifles to thaw them out. U.S. troops clung to icy roads as Chinese forces launched devastating attacks near the Chosin Reservoir.

On November 28, 1950, General Almond visited a battalion that survived the attack in those frozen mountains. The battalion was led by Lieutenant Colonel Don Carlos Faith Jr. Almond boasted, "We're still . . . going all the way to the Yalu." Then he pinned a Silver Star medal on Faith for gallantry (bravery) in action.

Faith knew his group would never make it to the Yalu River. As soon as Almond left, Faith ripped off the medal and flung it into the snow. Faith, his men, and a regiment whose leader was missing formed Task Force Faith. They ignored Almond's boast and began to fight their way back to the relative safety of Hagaru, twelve miles away.

Faith found a route across the frozen reservoir. He stayed back until his entire task force crossed, including vehicles carrying wounded soldiers. Then he ran forward and led his men through one deadly roadblock after another. On December 1, Faith was killed only about four miles from Hagaru. But 670 men made it to safety. The army later awarded Faith the Medal of Honor.

SOLDIERS AND UNIFORMS

The typical U.S. GI (short for "government issue") knew little about Korea and was not prepared for the extremes of heat and cold there.

In summer, U.S. soldiers in Korea wore
- Heavy leather combat boots
- Steel helmets
- Cotton shirts, pants, and fatigue caps

In winter they wore many layers:

Typical North Korean and Chinese soldiers wore
- Khaki or white quilted cotton uniforms
- Quilted cotton soft caps with ear flaps
- Soft, quilted boots

Marines stop at an icy roadblock in North Korea.

Eight huge C-119 transport planes each dropped a twenty-five-hundred-pound portion of a portable bridge into the chasm. A parachute-rigging team flew in from Japan to supervise the drop. Some of the pieces of the bridge crash-landed. But special army trucks were able to position four of them to make a barely usable bridge. The bridging work started on December 6. By the night of December 10, the last of the troops and tanks made it across. All this was done under constant enemy fire. The Koto-ri mission was so amazing and heroic that James Michener wrote a novel, *The Bridges at Toko-ri,* based on the heroic actions of U.S. troops during this dangerous phase of the war. His book was made into a popular movie.

"Gimme Tomorrow"

On a bitterly cold morning in early December 1950, a marine sat in the snow near Funchilin Pass eating breakfast. David Duncan, a photographer for *Life* magazine, took a picture of him chipping away at a can of frozen beans.

Duncan asked the marine, "If I were God, and I could give you anything you wanted, what would you ask for?"

The marine answered, "Gimme tomorrow."

In the meantime, military and political advisers in the United States worried about the war. The Chinese forces seemed unstoppable. The Eighth Army and X Corps were in full retreat. General MacArthur told the Joint Chiefs of Staff, "We face an entirely new war." He and others talked about losing Korea to the Communists or using the atomic bomb against China. On December 9, President Truman wrote in his diary, "I've worked for peace for five years and six months and it looks like World War III is here."

CROSSING THE PARALLEL AGAIN

At a conference with military officers on December 15, General Peng agreed that it was politically important for the Chinese People's Volunteers to cross the 38th Parallel. But it would be too difficult to supply the troops much farther south than that. Communist leaders in China and Korea were also worried about limiting the war. Fearing massive strikes in return, Mao Zedong did not let the Chinese Air Force attack UN targets, even though there were Chinese bombers stationed at bases in Manchuria.

But Mao was also determined to push U.S. forces out of Korea, especially because U.S. soldiers had caused the death of his son a few weeks earlier. Mao ignored General Peng's worries. He assured Kim Il Sung that, with China's help, Kim would soon rule over a united Korea, even though UN forces had better equipment and airpower. Mao's slogan was "Manpower will triumph over machines."

By December 15, all of the X Corps, including Smith's marines from Koto-ri, had made it to the port of Hungnam. Tanks ringed the city and aircraft provided a protective cover overhead. The remaining troops of X Corps and almost as many Korean refugees, as well as tons of equipment, were loaded onto navy ships. The ships headed south through the Sea of Japan. The last of the troops then blew up the port.

The Eighth Army also retreated into South Korea. Tens of thousands of refugees followed them. On December 23, the Eighth Army lost its commander, not to enemy fire but to a traffic accident. Racing in his jeep along an icy road, General Walker died in a head-on collision with a weapons carrier.

Far from being home for Christmas as General MacArthur had announced, U.S. troops had lost their offensive and seemed to be stuck where they had started months earlier.

RIDGWAY'S WAR

On January 4, General Peng and his troops attacked Seoul. UN forces again lost South Korea's capital to the Communists—as they

Escape

The evacuation from Hungnam was an immense undertaking. According to one historian, about 105,000 troops of the X Corps, plus all Communist and UN equipment worth taking—17,500 vehicles and 350,000 tons of supplies were loaded onto ships. About 98,000 refugees went on the ships too *(right)*.

Each person sailing from Hungnam had a different escape story. Chung Dong-kyu hid in the hold (cargo area) of a navy transport ship. Chung broke into an army truck on board to find something to eat. He found only dried, salted anchovies, which he gobbled down. "I was overcome with a powerful thirst . . . but my frantic search through that part of the ship turned up no drinking water."

For Eunice Coleman, a nurse aboard a hospital ship sailing with four hundred patients on Christmas Eve, escape meant "Christmas for everyone . . . a tree, Santa Claus . . . and a dance in the Operating Room."

As the last **UN** military personnel and Korean refugees left Hungnam, demolition charges blew up the harbor.

had the previous June. Was this the start of another retreat southward to Pusan? Not if General Walker's replacement could help it.

Lieutenant General Matthew Ridgway, the new commander of the Eighth Army, made it his business to put spirit back into his troops and to attack the Communist forces. A tough, no-nonsense soldier, he visited every unit on the front lines. Ridgway wore a medical kit strapped to one shoulder and a hand grenade strapped to the other. Under Ridgway, the Eighth Army spread over the hillsides instead of sticking to roads. Flares from C-47 planes lit up battlefields at night to make it easier to spot enemy soldiers. The Eighth Army

did so well that the army chief of staff announced to reporters that "as of now, we are going to stay and fight."

By the middle of January 1951, UN forces had stopped the Communist advance. Chinese troops also were suffering from the cold weather. They were short of ammunition and often lived off captured U.S. food supplies. The UN front lines held steady at about seventy-five miles south of Seoul. By the end of January, UN forces were back on the offensive.

Meanwhile, Chinese air force officers complained to their leaders, "If we [were allowed to provide] a strong air support, we could have driven the enemy into the sea." The Chinese planned a major offensive against UN troops in the spring. This time they wanted air support for their ground troops. The Chinese controlled Seoul's Kimpo Airfield. The Soviets had contributed hundreds of MiG jet fighters to the war effort. All that was needed was combat training for Chinese pilots.

FAST FACT

MERRY CHRISTMAS

One Christmas card that some U.S. soldiers sent to their friends at home started this way:

Xmas greetings from Korea
Land of lice and diarrhea.

General Liu Ya-lou, commander of China's air force, began a massive training program. The airspace between the Chongchon and Yalu Rivers in northwestern Korea became known as MiG Alley. Pilots for UN spy missions reported swarms of MiG fighters practicing there.

The cold, bleak month of February brought days when there was a lull in fighting and days when fighting was fierce. Soldiers slogged through the muck of rice paddies melting in an early spring thaw and fed by heavy rains. The worst battle for

the UN came in mid-February near Hoengsong. A large army of Chinese and North Korean soldiers attacked UN troops, forcing them to abandon Hoengsong and retreat farther south. The UN troops left behind arms and equipment, which their enemies later used against them. The South Koreans lost about ninety-eight hundred soldiers, the United States about nineteen hundred. A division of Dutch soldiers lost about one hundred men. This two-day battle holds the gruesome record for the highest num-

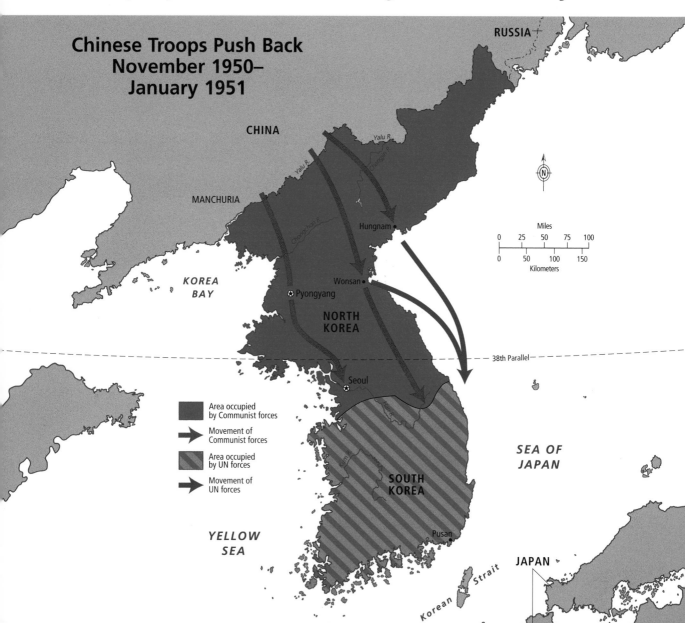

Chinese Troops Push Back November 1950– January 1951

RUSSIA

CHINA

Yalu R.

MANCHURIA

Hungnam

KOREA BAY

Wonsan

Pyongyang

NORTH KOREA

38th Parallel

Seoul

Area occupied by Communist forces

Movement of Communist forces

Area occupied by UN forces

Movement of UN forces

SEA OF JAPAN

SOUTH KOREA

YELLOW SEA

Pusan

Miles
0 25 50 75 100

0 50 100 150
Kilometers

JAPAN

Korean Strait

ber of U.S. Army deaths in the shortest amount of time during the Korean War.

Shortly after the battle for Hoengsong, General Ridgway launched Operation KILLER and Operation RIPPER. The goal of these military plans was to push enemy troops back over the 38th Parallel and to keep them from getting strong enough to mount another offensive. Naval ships started what would be an 861-day blockade of Wonsan Harbor in North Korea. UN planes began systematically bombing air bases in MiG Alley.

A thin supply line hampered Chinese forces, while UN troops received increasing supplies of equipment and fresh manpower. By March many of the Chinese soldiers in the front lines had died from cold, hunger, and disease as well as from UN firepower. Their replacements often had less than a month of basic training. Pounded by UN air strikes by day and artillery firing at night, the Chinese People's Volunteers began to retreat.

UN troops once again recaptured Seoul and headed toward the 38th Parallel. President Truman and other leaders of UN countries were ready to return to the UN's original mission—freedom for South Korea. Truman prepared a statement that he was willing to settle the conflict in Korea by peaceful means. Knowing that Truman planned to make this announcement, General MacArthur made an announcement first. Rather than calling for a discussion of peace between equal forces, MacArthur tried to humiliate China. He said that if UN restrictions were lifted, he would strike at China so viciously that the Chinese would be doomed.

This officer, with severe face and neck wounds, refused to leave the field until he finished evacuating the other wounded men of his company.

President Truman was furious. He knew that General MacArthur was very popular in the United States, but as Truman saw it, MacArthur had three strikes against him. First, he had violated a presidential order. It forbade military officers from commenting publicly on sensitive issues without permission from the Joint Chiefs of Staff. Second, MacArthur's warlike words made it impossible for leaders in China to push for an end to war. Mao would not surrender in light of such disrespect. Third, his announcement went completely against UN plans to seek peace.

By April 3, 1951, UN forces had crossed the 38th Parallel and moved back into North Korea—again. But President Truman decided that this time any war in North Korea would be waged without Douglas MacArthur, the man he had called our Big General in the Far East.

SETTING LIMITS

6

President Truman consulted with his political advisers and the Joint Chiefs of Staff. They agreed that General MacArthur would have to be relieved of his duties in Korea. The president arranged for Secretary of the Army Frank Pace Jr. to inform MacArthur personally before a public statement was made. But a Chicago newspaper found out about the firing. It planned to print the news on April 11. The White House wanted to be the first to announce MacArthur's firing, so it hastily prepared a statement for a press conference on April 10 at one in the morning.

General MacArthur hardly reacted, at least publicly, when the news reached him in Tokyo. For months he had contradicted his commander in chief about how to fight the Korean War. MacArthur could have

resigned in protest. But if he were fired, he thought, the American people might flock to support him. That might put him in a better position to run for president in 1952. MacArthur was a Republican, and he wanted to challenge Truman, a Democrat, for the presidency.

MacArthur had spent the past fourteen years fighting and leading military missions in Asia. At age seventy-one, he read the dismissal orders, turned to his wife, and said, "Jeannie, we're going home at last."

President Truman explained his actions on the radio. He praised MacArthur as "one of our greatest military commanders" but talked about the importance of a limited war. He said, "In the simplest terms, what we are doing in Korea is this: We are trying to prevent World War III. . . . It is essential to relieve General MacArthur so that there would be no doubt or confusion as to the real purpose and aim of our policy."

The firing of MacArthur shocked America. The general was a hero of World War II, a noble defender against Communism. In the first two days after Truman's announcement, the White House received 250,000 telegrams protesting his actions.

When MacArthur arrived in Washington, D.C., at midnight on April 19, 1951, all of the Joint Chiefs of Staff and many important members of Congress were there to greet him. President Truman was not.

MacArthur returned to a nation that was stirred up to an antiCommunist frenzy. Just ten days earlier, Judge Irving Kaufman

EYEWITNESS QUOTE:

"With deep regret I have concluded that General of the Army Douglas MacArthur is unable to give his wholehearted support to the policies of the United States Government and of the United Nations in matters pertaining to his official duties. . . . I have, therefore, relieved General MacArthur of his commands and have designated Lieutenant General Matthew B. Ridgway as his successor."

—President Harry S. Truman, April 10, 1951

handed down a death sentence to Julius and Ethel Rosenberg, who were convicted of spying for the Soviet Union. Americans believed in MacArthur's call for victory against Communism. They praised him and honored him with parades.

General MacArthur gave a dramatic speech to members of Congress. Millions of people listened in on the radio or watched the general on their black-and-white television sets. In his speech, MacArthur reminded Congress that he had served in the military for fifty-two years. He referred to an old song about how soldiers never die but just fade away. "And like that old soldier of that ballad," he said, "I now close my military career and just fade away—an old soldier who tried to do

Douglas MacArthur addresses Congress after he was fired by President Truman.

New York City held a grand parade to honor Douglas MacArthur.

his duty as God gave him the light to see that duty. Good-bye."

The Congress chamber erupted into applause. Congressman Dewey Short said of MacArthur, "We saw a great hunk of God in the flesh, and we heard the voice of God." President Truman remarked privately that MacArthur's speech "was nothing but a bunch of [expletive]."

Congress set up hearings to determine whether there were grounds for voting President Truman out of office. Some people insisted that Truman be fired instead of MacArthur. Others—including most major U.S. newspapers—thought Truman's actions upheld principles found in the Constitution. The Constitution clearly states that the United States is a country run by civilian leaders and not generals. People in bars and on commuter trains came to blows about whether Truman or MacArthur was right.

Leaders of the UN countries generally supported Truman's decision. They wanted to stick to a limited war, even if it meant firing General MacArthur.

VAN FLEET'S WAR

Unlike the song he quoted, General MacArthur was hardly fading away in the spring of 1951. Neither was the Korean War. General Ridgway replaced General MacArthur as UN commander. Lieutenant General James Van Fleet (he had become a full general in July) took Ridgway's place leading the Eighth Army. Van Fleet, like Mao Zedong, had lost a son in the Korean War.

By the time General Van Fleet took charge, there were about 580,000 UN troops in Korea, 229,000 of which were U.S. troops. General Peng's Chinese People's Volunteers numbered about 700,000. What the UN lacked in manpower, it made up for in airpower. Massive bombing assaults forced enemy troops back. In May Van Fleet also directed huge amounts of artillery fire at Chinese positions. "We must expend steel and fire, not men," he said. "I want so many artillery holes that a man can step from one to the other."

Since the UN troops were mostly south of the 38th Parallel, they were close to supply lines. They had recovered from the hardships of the winter. And starting in April, they got two morale boosters—rotations and R and R (rest and recreation). Soldiers earned a certain number of points each month depending on the level of danger they were in. For example, they received four points for being in a frontline combat zone and two points for being in a rear position. Soldiers who earned at least thirty-six points could leave Korea. Chinese soldiers also had a rotation system, but it was very different from the UN

system. Under the Chinese system, combat units rather than individual soldiers were rotated from the front lines to the rear every two to three months.

Besides the very popular rotation system, UN soldiers who had spent at least six months in Korea were allowed to spend five days of R and R at nearby bases in Japan. Hot showers, good food, and pleasant company did wonders for war-weary soldiers.

During the spring offensive and the UN counterattack, thousands upon thousands of Chinese and North Korean soldiers died or surrendered. Thousands of others retreated. By June 1951, UN forces held a line close to the 38th Parallel. The enemy armies ranged from about forty miles north of the 38th Parallel in the eastern part of Korea to a few miles below the Parallel in the west.

Rifle teams fire on Chinese positions near the 38th Parallel.

WEAPONS OF THE KOREAN WAR

Both the UN and Communist forces entered the Korean War using weapons that were available in World War II. Several of these weapons were replaced by newer models. Others remained in service throughout the war in Korea.

The United States provided most of the armaments used by UN forces in the Korean War. The Soviet Union provided most of the weapons for the Communist forces.

The basic weapon for UN forces was the U.S.-made M1 Garand rifle:
- semiautomatic (The trigger had to be pulled for each firing, but it could be fired continuously without reloading.)
- weight 9.5 lb.
- attachable bayonet
- rate of fire about 30 rounds/minute

Recruits in basic training at Fort Leonard Wood, Missouri, carry standard-issue M1 rifles.

Also widely used was the Browning automatic rifle (BAR):
- semiautomatic or fully automatic
- weight 16 lb.
- rate of fire 450–500 rounds/minute
- used same cartridge as the M1

Browning automatic rifle (BAR)

The basic machine gun used was the
M1919 (A-4) or light machine gun:
- fully automatic
- weight 32 lb.
- rate of fire 450–500 rounds/minute
- used the same cartridge as the
  M1 and BAR

M1919 (A-4)

The Chinese and North Korean forces relied heavily on a variety of infantry
rifles, all of simple design, very easy to maintain, and extremely rugged.

Another widely used Communist weapon was the Shpagin PPSH41 submachine gun:
- called the burp gun by UN forces because of the sound it makes
- semiautomatic or fully automatic
- weight 8 lb.
- rate of fire 700–900 rounds/minute
- inaccurate except at close range

Chinese troops often attacked first with hand grenades. A second wave of
troops would then attack with burp guns. Both sides often used fragmentation
grenades, which have an explosive charge in a metal case that breaks into deadly
flying fragments. These grenades could cause death within a range of 5–10 yards.

Other Weapons
- U.S. forces originally had anti-tank equipment (2.6-inch rocket launchers) that
  offered little defense against the Soviet T-34 tanks. These were replaced by the
  more effective 3.5-inch rocket launchers.
- The first jet-to-jet military battle in history took place over North Korea.
  Soviet-made MiG-15 jets challenged U.S.-made F-86 Sabre jets. The United
  States used straight-winged F-80 and F-84 jets as ground support.
- U.S. aircraft carriers were used mainly as airfields floating off the Korean
  coastline. Carrier-to-carrier battles, which were common in World War II, did
  not take place in Korea. UN naval forces included huge *Iowa*-class warships
  with large 16-inch guns, for offshore bombardment.
- The LSTs (landing ship tanks) that were used in the Inchon landing had
  originally carried Sherman tanks. Just before the landing, M26 Pershing tanks
  replaced the Shermans. These tanks were a better match for the Soviet-made
  T-34s. Few tank-to-tank clashes took place during the war.
- U.S. helicopters offered air support to ground forces as well as transportation
  for wounded soldiers to and from mobile hospitals.

The greatest arms threats of all were nuclear weapons that the United States
and the Soviet Union were designing. These weapons were never used.

TRUCE?

American public opinion began to switch from MacArthur's push for complete victory to favor President Truman's idea of a limited war. The time seemed right to settle matters and bring the troops home. The Joint Chiefs of Staff instructed Van Fleet not to push deeply into North Korea. Diplomats put out "feelers" (dropped hints) to Chinese and Soviet leaders that the United States and the United Nations—although not South Korea—were willing to accept a truce line near the 38th Parallel.

On June 23, Jacob Malik, the Soviet delegate to the UN, said that "discussions should be started between the belligerents [warring nations] for a cease-fire and an armistice providing for the mutual withdrawal of forces from the 38th Parallel." An armistice is a temporary end to fighting. It usually happens while both sides in war try to work out a peace agreement.

A few days later, President Truman instructed General Ridgway to meet with Chinese and North Korean commanders. They agreed to meet three miles south of the 38th Parallel at Kaesong, the former capital of Korea. The first truce teams met on July 8. At the suggestion of the Communist leaders, the UN team arrived with white flags on their jeeps. The photos in Communist newspapers made it look like the UN forces were surrendering.

July 10, 1951, marked the first meeting of complete delegations from opposing sides in the Korean War. Although set in a peaceful teahouse, the truce talks were filled with squabbles, distrust, and frustration. During one deadlock, both sides glared at each other in silence for two hours and ten

Members of the North Korean–Chinese cease-fire delegation

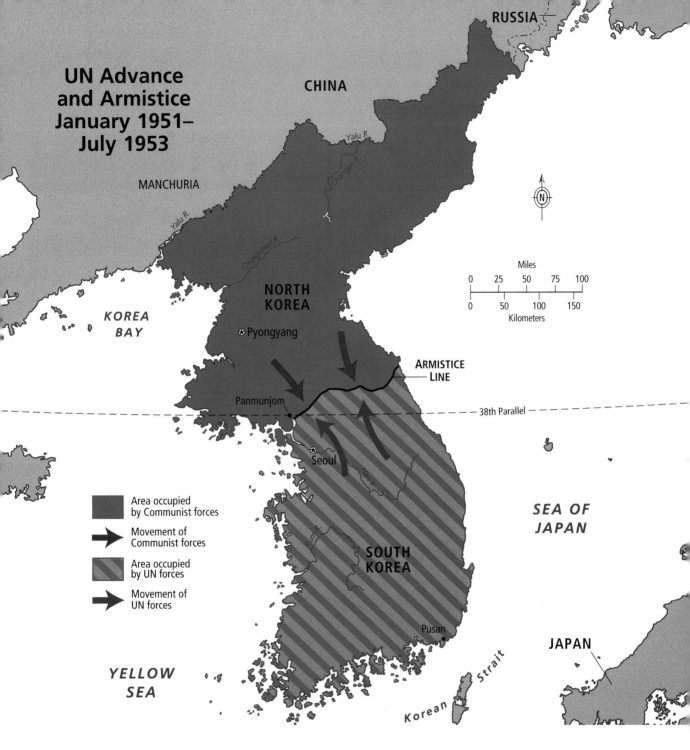

UN Advance and Armistice January 1951– July 1953

RUSSIA

CHINA

MANCHURIA

Yalu R.

Changjin R.

Yalu R.

Chong-chon R.

NORTH KOREA

KOREA BAY

⊛ Pyongyang

ARMISTICE LINE

Panmunjom

38th Parallel

⊛ Seoul

Han R.

Kum R.

SOUTH KOREA

SEA OF JAPAN

Pusan

JAPAN

YELLOW SEA

Korean Strait

Miles

0 25 50 75 100

0 50 100 150

Kilometers

N

Area occupied by Communist forces

Movement of Communist forces

Area occupied by UN forces

Movement of UN forces

minutes. On August 22, the Communist delegation charged that a UN warplane had bombed Kaesong and tried to kill them. They suspended the talks.

The UN and Communist delegations to these talks had genuine disputes about what should be done in Korea. But as events later showed, the Communist leaders were also stalling for time. A relative lull in the fighting during the summer of 1951 gave them a chance to strengthen their badly battered forces.

B-26 bombers hit a North Korean railroad yard.

During the summer, the UN forces carried out Operation STRANGLE—massive air strikes meant to choke off supplies to North Korean and Chinese troops. United Nations planes bombed highways and bridges, truck convoys, and trains. In one air assault in August, 35 B-29 bombers struck railroad lines in a North Korean port only nineteen miles from the Soviet Union.

Despite these attacks, the North Koreans managed to keep their supply lines going. Thousands of people filled craters, cleared debris, and erected temporary bridges, sometimes within hours of an attack. UN pilots took daytime surveys of enemy trucks and trains that were destroyed. But many of those supposedly destroyed vehicles were able to be operated secretly at night.

MiG Alley came alive with enemy planes in September. Each day as many as ninety MiG jet fighters flew across the Yalu River to attack the UN fighters. The pilots clearly had trained well, but the UN maintained control of the skies.

EYEWITNESS QUOTE:
OPERATION STRANGLE

"There's an air strike going on about 3 miles up the road. . . the Air Force and Artillery are giving us fits with their noise. This place we are in now is a horrifying sight. We can't turn around without sighting dead men or horses."

—a U.S. platoon sergeant, June 1951

Mud and Mortar

Before UN troops advanced up a hill, a mortar company often pounded the hillside with artillery fire. Charles Woods describes what it was like to fire the big guns:

A mortar crew fires on Communist positions.

> This is how we fought. We stood by our guns night and day.... We shoveled our way behind with just enough room [to crouch down] behind the gun and fire. The paint on our [mortar] tubes peeled, we burned our hands, we kept up the fire....
>
> We wolfed down C [rations] and relieved ourselves in a pit.... We were deafened by our own guns. Our eyes burned; our heads ached like someone sticking hot needles in the brain.
>
> The rain stopped, and everything dried up. Our muddy footprints became traps for those too tired to lift their feet. Mud dried to dust and blew in our eyes, and everyone had dirty faces streaked with sweat. No one could remember how long we had been there.
>
> On the eighth day the hill was secure.

With truce talks still suspended, UN troops inched their way northward. Artillery and air bombardments pelted enemy troops. By October the Communists were ready to resume truce talks. Both sides met at Panmunjom, a deserted village of four mud huts about five miles west of Kaesong. On October 25, more than three months after the talks first started, the delegations once again met. This time the site was a military tent instead of a teahouse.

Hopes ran high for bringing the troops home soon. No one knew then that the final armistice was still more than one year and many thousands of deaths away. This was the start of what many people called the talking war.

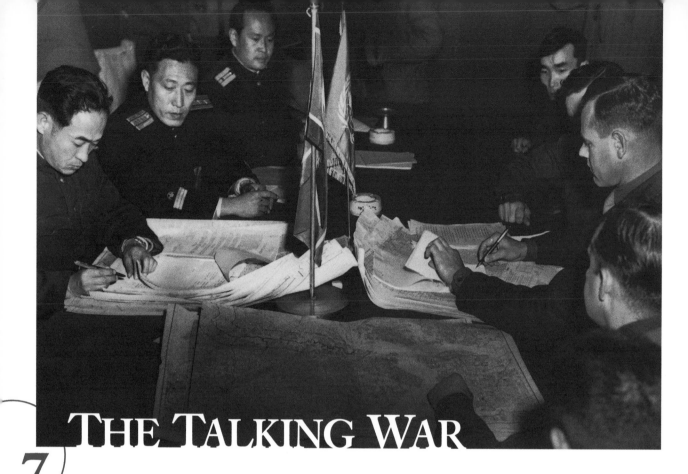

THE TALKING WAR

7

Starting in late October 1951, the UN and Communist delegations pushed each other toward a truce. Vice Admiral C. Turner Joy, a U.S. naval officer, headed the UN delegation in Panmunjom. South Korea's General Paik Sun Yup attended only as an observer. General Nam Il, who was chief of staff of the North Korean army, headed the Communist delegation. But Nam took his cues from Hsieh Fang, chief of staff of the Chinese army. The fate of Korea was really in the hands of the United States, China, and in the background, the Soviet Union.

The talks involved four goals that later became the four major sections, or articles, in the armistice agreement. Article I focused on establishing a final line (known as the demarcation line) between the opposing armies and a demilitarized zone (DMZ) where military operations were banned. Article II concerned the supervision of the armistice once an agreement was signed. Article III covered the exchange of POWs. Article IV called for a political conference on Korea after the military issues were settled.

While the truce talks dragged on, Chinese and North Korean soldiers dug in, too. From October 1951 through the spring of 1953, the soldiers spent much of their time in expertly built tunnels, bunkers, and deep trenches. Many of the tunnels had entrances on the protected side of a hill and exits facing the UN lines.

Starting in November, General Ridgway ordered an "active defense" strategy for UN ground troops. Rather than mounting major offensives, UN forces attempted to hold their ground. They advanced or retreated by only a few hundred yards, rather than miles. Battles raged over hills that often had military names based on how high they were. But to U.S. soldiers who fought to keep them or lost them to enemy forces, the hills took on names like Old Baldy and Heartbreak Ridge.

On November 27, 1951, the negotiators arranged the Little Armistice. This was an agreement to cease fire for thirty days along the front. During this time, formal talks began on exchanging prisoners. Both sides published lists of soldiers they had captured. Thousands of UN soldiers who were missing in action or who had been taken prisoner were not on the Communist list. The North Koreans also claimed that more than fifty thousand South Koreans had been "released at the front." Relief at having a list gave way to grief at the number of soldiers not on it.

Talks during the Little Armistice failed to resolve the POW issues or any others. On December 27, artillery started booming again. Both sides had agreed that some troops could be replaced along the front lines, so that both armies could maintain their effectiveness in fighting. However, the Chinese used the Little Armistice as they used other lulls in fighting—to rebuild and strengthen their army.

UN POWs wait for an agreement on prisoner exchange.

MEDICAL CARE

Bad weather and rapidly changing battle lines made it hard to provide good medical care to UN troops during the first year of the Korean War. Even so, UN soldiers got better medical treatment than enemy troops. A smaller percentage of U.S. soldiers died of their wounds during the Korean War than during World War II.

Mobile Army Surgical Hospital (MASH) units saved many lives. Several UN countries set them up close to the front lines. During the first year of the war, a MASH might move with the troops dozens of times. As battle lines became settled, a MASH might move only two or three times a year.

At first, the MASH units provided only emergency surgery to soldiers. But they quickly became small all-purpose hospitals. Helicopters, which were first used to pick up downed pilots, soon flew wounded soldiers to and from MASH units. Although a MASH was designed to hold about sixty patients, it often held hundreds. Often there were too few doctors and nurses to handle the overwhelming numbers of wounded soldiers brought from the battlefields. Later in the war, medical experts visited MASH units and taught new techniques to the personnel. But in the beginning, the medical staff often learned how to treat war injuries on the job.

MASH evacuation helicopter and medical personnel

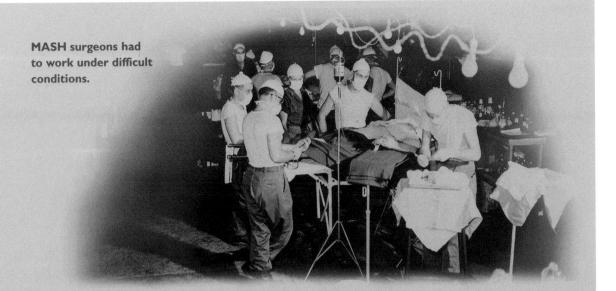

MASH surgeons had to work under difficult conditions.

A MASH tent provided little protection from the bitter winter weather. Blood plasma froze, ice-clogged generators broke down, and surgeons worked by flashlight. A MASH wasn't all that comfortable in the sweltering summer heat, either.

The 8055 MASH became the basis for the television series *M*A*S*H*. Luluah Houseknecht was an 8055 MASH nurse in 1950. She says, "We never had time to do all the playing they did on TV. . . . If we weren't busy taking care of the patients, we were packing up and moving on."

Medical care also included field hospitals (based just behind the front lines) and regular hospitals in South Korea or elsewhere. Most patients were carried to field hospitals in ambulances or on hospital trains and hospital ships. Airplanes bringing supplies or mail from Japan would likely carry thirty to eighty patients on stretchers back to hospitals in Japan on the return trip.

Soldiers suffered from more than battle wounds. Dysentery and frostbite were common. Starting in the spring of 1951, UN troops suffered outbreaks of viral hemorrhagic fever, in which patients die from internal bleeding. Neither the cause nor a cure was found during the war. At first, the death rate from the disease was 1 person in 5. As treatment improved, the death rate dropped to 1 in 50.

North Korean and Chinese soldiers had fewer medical services. Helicopter and MASH teams were not available to assist them. It was difficult to get medical supplies to their front lines because of UN bombing raids. By early 1951, battlefield medical services seemed to have collapsed. Thousands died of poorly treated wounds and diseases brought on by extreme cold, poor sanitary conditions, and other causes. Soldiers also suffered from typhus, a deadly disease, which likely came from an outbreak in Manchuria, north of the Yalu River. The Communists claimed that the United States purposely introduced typhus into the battlefield. But there is no evidence that this was true.

This cartoon published in a U.S. magazine in 1952 shows "talk" graves illustrating the number of lives lost as the peace talks dragged on.

SHAKY AGREEMENTS

The truce talks improved for a while early in 1952. Both sides agreed to what would become Article IV. They recommended that within three months after the armistice agreement took effect, a political conference would be held "to settle through negotiation the questions of the withdrawal of all foreign forces from Korea, the peaceful settlement of the Korean question, et cetera."

At the end of March, President Truman announced that he would not run again for president in the upcoming November elections. He was not popular. Americans were frustrated with the talking war in Korea.

At the end of April, negotiators came to a shaky agreement on Article II about supervising the armistice. Actions in both North and South Korea would be monitored by a UN team—the Neutral Nations Supervisory Commission—from Czechoslovakia, Poland, Sweden, and Switzerland. Only Switzerland was politically neutral. It had no ties to either side in the Cold War. Czechoslovakia and Poland were firmly in the grip of the Soviet Union. Sweden sided with the UN.

Meanwhile, two great World War II generals were competing for a chance to be president of the United States. General Dwight D. Eisenhower, hero of the Allied campaign in Europe, challenged General MacArthur for the Republican nomination for president. Eisenhower won. General Ridgway left Korea and took over Eisenhower's post as commander of NATO. General Mark Clark took over Ridgway's place as supreme commander of the UN forces in Korea. Just as General Clark began his command in Korea, Admiral Joy left the truce talks in Panmunjom. Lieutenant General William Harrison took his place.

NATO

The North Atlantic Treaty Organization was founded in 1949, during the Cold War, to safeguard the freedom of the community of nations bordering the North Atlantic Ocean. An armed attack on any NATO nation was considered an attack on them all. NATO members included Western European countries, Canada, and the United States. NATO also encouraged economic and political cooperation among its members.

FAST FACT

The Night Before Christmas

Leonard Hastings, a U.S. soldier in Korea during the talking war, sent this to his wife:

"Night Before Christmas"

It was the night before Christmas and all through
the tent
Was the odor of fuel oil (the stovepipe was bent).
The shoelaces were hung by the fireplace with care
In hopes that they'd issue each G.I. a new pair.
The weary G.I.'s were sacked out in their beds,
And vision of sugar babes danced through their heads.
When up on the ridgeline there rose such a clatter,
(A Chinese machine gun had started to chatter.)
I rushed to my rifle and threw back the bolt,
The rest of my tent-mates awoke with a jolt.
Outside we could hear our Platoon Sergeant Kelly,
A hard little man with a little pot belly.
"Come Yancey, come Clancey, come Connors,
and Watson,
Up Miller, up Baker, and Dodson."
We tumble outside in a swirl of confusion,
So cold that each man could have used a transfusion.
"Get up on that hilltop and silence the 'Red [enemy],'
And don't come back 'til you're sure that he's dead."
Then, putting his thumb up in front of his nose,
Sergeant Kelly took leave of us shivering Joes.
But we all heard him say in a voice soft and light,
"Merry Christmas to all, may you live through the night."

A U.S. soldier uses his poncho to protect himself from the bitter Korean winter.

Soon after President Truman announced that he would leave office in January 1953, the Communist delegation at Panmunjom began to object to almost everything. They hoped to get a better deal from the next president. U.S. political and military leaders were losing patience. At the end of June, the U.S. Air Force and Navy launched a massive air attack on the Suiho Dam on the North Korean side of the Yalu River. The hydroelectric plant at the dam supplied power to all of North Korea and some power to Chinese-held Manchuria. The planes made more than fourteen hundred bombing runs in three days, crippling the generating plant.

British political leaders worried that the United States was going to extend the war. They raised their objections to U.S. officials, but the bombing raids continued throughout North Korea. The Joint Chiefs of Staff explained that they wanted to pressure the Communists "to make an armistice a matter of urgency."

From one point of view, there really was a new urgency to end the war. The United States tested its first hydrogen bomb on November 1, 1952. This new bomb was one thousand times more deadly than the atomic bombs dropped on Japan in World War II. U.S. military leaders knew that Soviet scientists were not far behind with their own hydrogen bomb experiments. A UN naval task force was secretly equipped with much smaller nuclear weapons, in case the war extended to more countries. If the Cold War turned into an active all-out war, world destruction was a possibility.

But nothing looked particularly urgent on the ground in Korea. Battle lines were fairly stable. Both armies fired artillery at each other, fought from time to time, and patrolled each other's front lines constantly. They set up loudspeakers and broadcast propaganda messages to one another.

Dwight D. Eisenhower won the presidential election in November. Once the Communists knew that the next president

The world's first hydrogen bomb was tested on a remote island in the South Pacific on November 1, 1952.

of the United States would be an anti-Communist military leader, talks at Panmunjom improved for a while. The delegations agreed to the basics of Article I. They decided that the demarcation line between the two enemy armies would be based on battlefield positions and that both sides would retreat enough to form a demilitarized zone 2.5 miles wide and 250 miles long between them.

Shortly after his election, President-elect Eisenhower kept a campaign promise he had made to go to Korea. He visited leaders and troops for three days. But Eisenhower didn't come up with answers to the stalemate at the truce talks.

New Year's Day 1953 came and went, and the war slogged on. In February Lieutenant General Maxwell Taylor took General Van Fleet's place leading the Eighth Army. Battle lines hardly budged. Neither did the armistice negotiators.

FINALLY

The main sticking point at Panmunjom was Article III—prisoner exchange. Of the 130,000 or so North Korean and Chinese prisoners held in the UN's POW camps, somewhere between 22,000 and 75,000 (according to various counts) wanted to stay in South Korea when they were freed. The Communist delegation demanded that prisoners be repatriated (returned to their home countries), even by force. Britain had no problem with forced repatriation. After World War II, thousands of Soviet POWs in Germany were returned against their will to the Soviet Union. But President Truman insisted that repatriation be voluntary.

Fulfilling a campaign pledge, president-elect Dwight Eisenhower *(left)* visits the troops in Korea.

Soviet leader Joseph Stalin encouraged the Communists to take a hard line on the prisoner exchange issue. If the United States was still bogged down in Korea, it couldn't shift all of its attention to Soviet-designed Communist political activity in Western Europe. Also, he liked the idea that the prisoner issue created tension between the United States and Great Britain.

Pork Chop Hill

The first U.S. troops to take Pork Chop Hill called it Outpost 13. Pork Chop Hill was not the hill's real name, of course. But to U.S. soldiers, the hill looked like a pork chop. It was not far from The T-Bone.

Pork Chop Hill is part of a chain of low hills just north of the 38th Parallel. These hills overlook a valley that for centuries has been part of an invasion route into southern Korea. The route leads directly to Seoul.

During the second half of the war, the line between U.S. and Chinese forces barely moved. That line ran very close to Pork Chop Hill, and both sides were determined to have it. In April 1953, U.S. soldiers bravely held the hill against brutal enemy attacks. Losses were heavy. Since Pork Chop Hill lies just north of the demilitarized zone, U.S. forces finally abandoned the hill in July, as part of the truce agreement. The battle for Pork Chop Hill was later the subject of a popular movie.

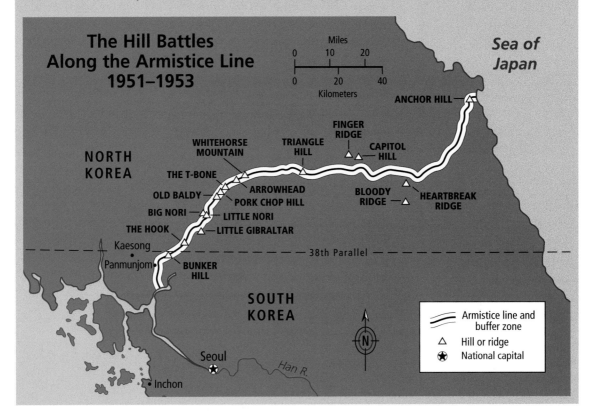

A released U.S. prisoner of war steps out of a Communist truck at Panmunjom.

On March 5, 1953, Stalin died. About three weeks later, with the Soviet Union suffering from political problems at home and China unwilling to maintain a costly war, the Communist delegation suddenly agreed to voluntary repatriation. In late April, each side began the first POW switch, the Little Switch. The UN returned about 6,670 sick or wounded prisoners. The Communists returned only 684.

An armistice seemed so close—and yet somehow there was always another sticking point. At the end of May, the UN delegation presented its absolutely final terms for truce. The delegation threatened a full-scale war if these terms weren't accepted. President Eisenhower hinted that the United States might use nuclear weapons against China.

But in June, it was South Korea's President Rhee—not the Communists—who stopped the peace process. Rhee pulled his troops out of the UN's Eighth Army. His supporters staged bitter anti-American protests. And in a move meant to anger the Communists, Rhee freed about twenty-seven thousand North Korean and Chinese prisoners and asked the South Koreans to give them shelter.

Rhee argued that the United States and General MacArthur had promised to

EYEWITNESS QUOTE:

"Both the Communists and the South Korean government have raised so many difficulties in the . . . negotiations intended to end the fighting that it raises in my mind a serious question as to whether or not the United Nations will ever again go into an arena to protect the inhabitants against Communist attack."

—President Dwight Eisenhower, July 24, 1953

General William Harrison *(left)* and North Korean general Nam Il *(right)* sat at separate tables to sign the armistice agreement.

reunite all of Korea under his government. But at the truce talks, the United States and the UN were willing to settle for a limited victory in a limited war. General MacArthur's policies no longer mattered.

The truce talks stalled, but the Communists did not renew their war effort. The United States agreed to help Rhee rebuild the South Korean army and to provide long-term economic aid. The talks resumed on July 10, exactly two years after they had formally started at Kaesong.

EYEWITNESS QUOTE: CEASE-FIRE

"The cease-fire caused a measure of anguish in the officers and men of the Korean army, because it perpetuated the division of our nation. . . . The killing stopped at last. . . . So many of my subordinates had been killed that I literally could not count them."

—South Korean general Paik Sun Yup, 1953

As the final details were drawn up for a truce, both armies fought hard. The demarcation line was to be based on the position of the front lines at the time of the armistice. Each side wanted to get a better position.

On July 27, 1953, at 10:00 in the morning, the delegations walked into a small building—Panmunjom's "peace pagoda"—made of tar paper and straw matting. Lieutenant General William Harrison (Admiral Joy's replacement) came without a tie or his military medals. General Nam Il was in full dress uniform. Each man

U.S. soldiers celebrate news of the armistice agreement.

sat at a separate table and signed nine copies of the main armistice agreement— three copies in English, three in Chinese, and three in Korean. The UN copies had blue covers, and the Communist copies had red covers. Under President Rhee's orders, no South Korean signed the armistice.

Some say that when Harrison and Nam finished signing, they glanced at each other. Others say that they didn't. We do know that they did not say a word and simply got up and walked out. The truce talks, which had lasted more than two years—two years in which many more lives were lost—were over, without ceremony, in ten minutes.

EPILOGUE

UN soldiers in Korea heard the news of the armistice in nine different languages. They cheered or smiled, but mostly they took the news quietly. Twelve hours after the armistice agreement was signed, the fighting in Korea officially stopped.

Back in the United States, some people celebrated in the streets, but there were no cheering throngs and wild celebrations as there had been after World War II. This was a war many Americans found confusing. They wondered what we had won in Korea.

President Eisenhower spoke on television about his relief that the military conflict was over. He also said that Korea was "an armistice on a single battleground, not

peace in the world. We may not now relax our guard nor cease our quest."

The next day, the Military Armistice Commission held its first meeting to figure out how the armistice would work. The commission was made up of ten countries that were members of the United Nations Command in Korea. Their job included managing activities in the demilitarized zone and working with the Neutral Nations Supervisory Commission (Switzerland, Sweden, Poland, and Czechoslovakia) to bring about a permanent peace between North and South Korea.

The main prisoner of war exchange—the Big Switch—started on August 5. For the next month, soldiers passed through

Panmunjom on their way back to their home countries. The UN handed over about seventy-six thousand North Korean and Chinese POWs. More than twenty-two thousand other UN prisoners decided not to go back. The Communists returned about thirteen thousand POWs, including about thirty-six hundred U.S. soldiers. About three hundred sixty UN soldiers in Communist camps refused to return home, including twenty-three U.S. soldiers.

Prisoners who were returned to the UN Command went to a place near Panmunjom called Freedom Village. They were treated for lice, given new clothes, and questioned about life in the prison camps. The last of the prisoners of war finally went

home around Christmas 1953, three years after General MacArthur's promised Christmas 1950 end to the conflict.

From POW reports, life was gruesome in the Communist prison camps. Thousands of POWs died from cruel treatment and starvation. U.S. prisoners were also subjected to brainwashing—a painful mix of propaganda and mental torture—and some of these prisoners wound up giving military information to their captors.

Most of the prisoners in UN camps were treated better than POWs in Communist camps. They had enough to eat and sufficient clothing. Some South Korean civilians even sneaked into camps

Billy Shaw

Henry McDermott survived fourteen months in a Chinese prison camp thanks to Billy Shaw, a nineteen-year-old African American soldier from a poor family in Texas. "Because of [fever] and diarrhea, I couldn't get up off the floor to eat. . . . He used to sit me up three times a day and hand feed me my rice rations. Billy . . . prechewed all the rice to make it softer for me to swallow." Shaw was beaten and killed one day at camp for singing "God Bless America."

to get free food. But life in these camps was sometimes brutal too. Nationalist Chinese guards from Taiwan (which was a UN member) tried to "persuade" the Chinese prisoners to give up Communism and go to Taiwan. And some of the UN camps were in reality run by the Communist prisoners themselves, who kept other prisoners in line by torturing or killing them.

The UN Command tried to take control of its camps away from both the Communist prisoners and the anti-Communist Nationalist Chinese guards. This was important in part because the UN delegation at the truce talks wanted to get an accurate count of how many Communist prisoners did not want to return home. But gaining control of the POW camps was not easy. In May 1952, prisoners at the Koje-do camp seized the camp's UN commander—Brigadier General Francis Dodd—and threatened to kill him. Dodd was freed only after another camp commander signed a false confession stating that "many [prisoners of war] have been killed and wounded by UN forces."

DRAWING THE LINE ONCE AGAIN

The armistice agreement fixed the demarcation line between the two enemy armies near the 38th Parallel, close to where it had been before North Korea invaded in 1950. South Korea gained 2,350 square miles of North Korean territory in the western half of the peninsula. North Korea added 850 square miles south of the 38th Parallel in the eastern half. The demilitarized zone around the demarcation line was 2.5 miles

Communist fighters captured by South Korean troops are fed in a POW camp.

Korean civilians killed by retreating North Korean troops were thrown into trenches.

wide and 155 miles long. Because very few people crossed the DMZ, the area became a sort of nature preserve for plants and animals.

About four million people were wounded or killed during the fighting in Korea. Half of them were civilians. About 3.7 million children lost their parents. Millions more Koreans, unable to cross between North and South Korea, became separated from their families. According to official records, 36,516 U.S. soldiers died in the Korean War. Of these, 33,686 died in battle and 2,830 died from disease or other causes.

After three years of intense fighting up and down the peninsula, Korea was in ruins. The land was battle-scarred and burned. Cities were bombed into rubble. Practically everything had to be rebuilt.

Some U.S. soldiers remain in South Korea to advise the South Korean military, to help them rebuild, and to maintain the DMZ. Most U.S. soldiers returned home, where they were usually greeted with respect and relief—not as heroes but as men and women who carried out their duties. Some men also returned home with war brides—Korean women they had married. These women were the first Koreans allowed to enter the United States legally since 1924. The ban on immigration from Korea was formally lifted in 1952.

As President Eisenhower noted, the armistice agreement was not a peace treaty. It was merely a temporary arrangement to stop the fighting. But as month after month went by, the political conference proposed in Article IV of the armistice agreement failed to take place. During the rest of 1953 and early 1954, political leaders in the UN, as well as China and North Korea, met to discuss a final settlement of the war. They agreed that the question of what would happen in Korea would be answered at a conference in Geneva, Switzerland, in April 1954. But that conference also proved to be a failure. The members of the conference could not establish a peace that would bring a real end to a conflict that had never even been declared a war.

THE HOME FRONT

Americans first thought that the conflict in Korea was a necessary, swift, and sure way to stop the expansion of Communism in Asia. We had somehow "lost" China to the Communist government of Mao Zedong, and we would have to draw the line at Korea. In general, Americans approved of President Truman's position. They echoed General Eisenhower's statement that the United States would "have a dozen Koreas soon if we don't take a firm stand."

Most people believed General MacArthur's statements that he would win the war, unite Korea under a democratic government, and bring the troops home by Christmas 1950. Most people on the home front knew little about Korea and assumed that America's superior technology would triumph.

As war-weary veterans of World War II were called back to active duty and young men were drafted into military service, the mood on the home front began to change. Newspapers and magazines reported on the brutal conditions of war in Korea. When President Truman fired General MacArthur for widening the war, Americans were divided over who was right. But even MacArthur supporters lost their enthusiasm as the war dragged on.

The people at home began to feel the economic pinch of a war-time economy. Taxes went up. As materials went to the war effort, some consumer products were hard to find. Wages and prices were frozen to prevent inflation.

Americans became more and more dissatisfied. During the 1952 elections, Republicans blamed Democrats for Communism, corruption, and Korea. Korea had become, as one soldier put it, "the war we can't win, we can't lose, we can't quit." It wasn't until July 1953 that the fighting ended, and POWs were released and the troops came home.

This illustration, which appeared in a U.S. newspaper in April 1953, is entitled "Endless Night." The image symbolized families waiting for their sons and daughters to come home as the war and peace negotiations dragged on.

In one sense, the situation in Korea at the end of the war was almost exactly as it had been before the invasion three years earlier. Two separate nations remained—a Communist one in North Korea and a more democratic one in South Korea. Both of these nations started out fighting for a total victory, one in which all of Korea would be united under one government. But both sides had to settle for less, because their more powerful allies were unwilling to fight for more.

The Korean War did bring about other changes. Communist China became a nation to be reckoned with because it had stood up to the United States. The UN proved that it would respond with force to a military attack on one of its members. Tensions increased between the Communist countries of China and the Soviet Union on one side and the nonCommunist countries of Western Europe and the United States on the other. The old alliances that held through World War II shifted to new alliances in this war, one of the first major conflicts of the Cold War era. The United States grew closer to former enemies—Japan and Germany—in an effort to contain the expansion of its former ally—the Soviet Union.

General Matthew Ridgway wrote a book about his experiences in Korea. He called the conflict there "the forgotten war." But those who fought in Korea never forgot

> **EYEWITNESS QUOTE:**
>
> **"The cold and the heat, that's what I remember the most about Korea. Forget the bugs, the steep hills, the horrible food, being shot at, and the dysentery; it was the cold and the heat I remember."**
>
> **—U.S. Sergeant Thomas McLain**

their experiences there. Some wondered what the purpose of the war had been or wished that the end of the war had brought as clear a victory as U.S. forces had gained in World War II.

U.S. troops remain in South Korea. Fourteen thousand troops guard the DMZ, and others are posted elsewhere in the country. Over the years, the DMZ, without any human population, has become a kind of wildlife refuge.

In 1994 former U.S. president Jimmy Carter met with North Korean officials and worked out an agreement that North Korea refrain from further development of nuclear weapons. In 2003 North Korea announced that it was resuming nuclear weapons programs and demanded to negotiate the matter directly with the United States. President George W. Bush insisted that other nations in the area be involved. At the same time, North and South Korea were moving slowly toward opening the border between them, and there were protests in South Korea, demanding the removal of U.S. troops.

In 2003 the United States decided to move U.S. troops from the DMZ. New methods of war, with long-range missiles and long-distance bombing, meant that soldiers no longer needed to be stationed so close to the line of possible battle. The war that Douglas MacArthur predicted would end by Christmas 1950 is still without a peace treaty and a unified Korea.

MAJOR BATTLES OF THE KOREAN WAR

Seoul Falls to Communists	June 28, 1950
Taejon Falls to Communists	July 21, 1950
Inchon Invasion—Operation CHROMITE	September 15–16, 1950
Pusan Perimeter Breakout	September 16–28, 1950
Seoul Recaptured	September 28, 1950
Wonsan Captured by South Korean Troops	October 10, 1950
Pyongyang Falls	October 19, 1950
First Jet-to-Jet Air Battle	November 8, 1950
Chosin Reservoir Attack	November 27, 1950
General Oliver Smith's Bridge at Koto-ri	December 8–10, 1950
Last UN Troops Leave North Korea from Hungnam	December 24, 1950
Seoul Falls to Communists (again)	January 4, 1951
UN Troops Recapture Seoul (again)	March 14, 1951
The Hill Battles Near 38th Parallel (see p. 68)	June 1951–July 1953
Battle of Pork Chop Hill	April–July, 1953

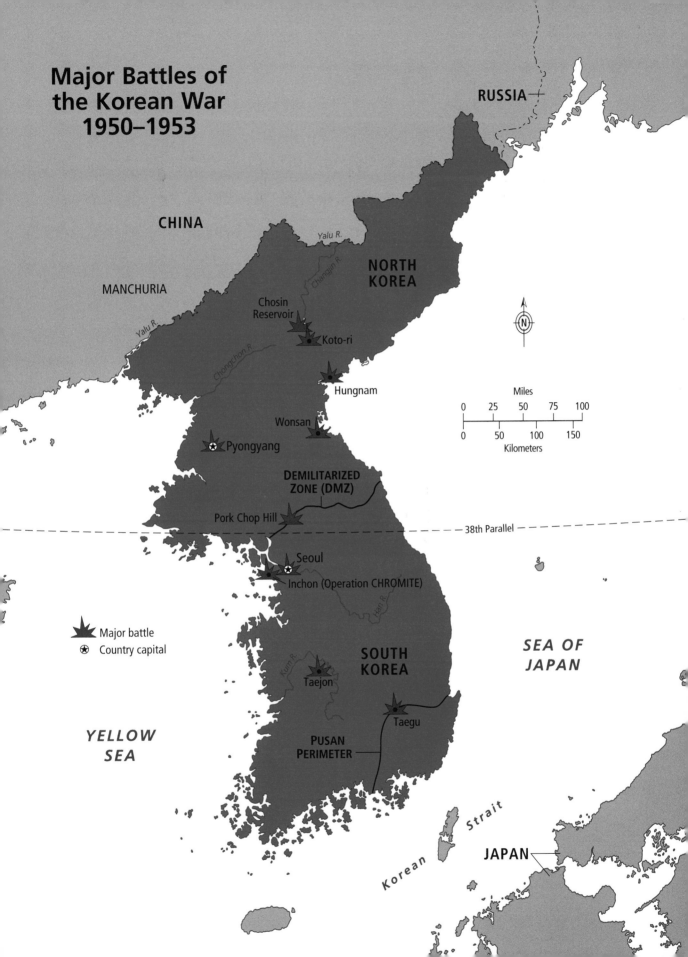

Major Battles of the Korean War 1950–1953

RUSSIA

CHINA

MANCHURIA

Yalu R.

Changjin R.

NORTH KOREA

Chosin Reservoir

Koto-ri

Chongchon R.

Yalu R.

Hungnam

Wonsan

✪ Pyongyang

N

DEMILITARIZED ZONE (DMZ)

Miles
0   25   50   75   100

0   50   100   150
Kilometers

Pork Chop Hill

38th Parallel

✪ Seoul

Inchon (Operation CHROMITE)

Han R.

SEA OF JAPAN

★ Major battle
✪ Country capital

SOUTH KOREA

Kum R.

Taejon

Taegu

PUSAN PERIMETER

YELLOW SEA

Korean Strait

JAPAN

KOREAN WAR TIMELINE

1950   North Korean troops cross the 38th Parallel and capture Seoul, June 25–28.

President Truman commits U.S. ground troops to fight in Korea, June 30.

U.S. forces capture Inchon, September 15–16.

UN troops break out of Pusan Perimeter and recapture Seoul, September 16–28.

First jet-to-jet air combat in history, November 8.

Chinese troops push UN troops in North Korea southward, November–December.

Eighth Army commander dies; General Matthew Ridgway takes command, December 23.

Last UN troops evacuate from port of Hungnam, December 24.

1951   Seoul falls to Communist forces, January 4.

UN troops retake Seoul, March 14.

President Truman relieves General MacArthur of duty; General Ridgway takes command, April 10.

Fighting stalls near the 38th Parallel, June–July.

Soviet diplomat Jacob Malik proposes cease-fire, June 23.

Peace talks begin at Kaesong, July 10.

Peace talks resume at a new site—Panmunjom, October 25.

1952   UN forces bomb Suiho power plant, June 23–24.

Dwight Eisenhower elected president of the United States, November 4.

1953   Soviet leader Joseph Stalin dies, March 5.

Battle of Pork Chop Hill begins April 16.

Operation Little Switch (prisoner exchange) begins April 20.

Armistice is signed at Panmunjom, July 27.

Operation Big Switch, August–December.

As of 2003   No permanent peace treaty is signed.

GLOSSARY

armistice: a temporary end to fighting by a formal agreement of warring armies

artillery: mounted guns or missile launchers. Artillery may be light or heavy, depending on the size of the object that is fired.

bunker: a chamber built partially underground, often made of steel, concrete, and other strong materials. Soldiers use bunkers as protected places from which to fire on the enemy.

cease-fire: an order or agreement for enemy armies to stop firing on each other. A cease-fire is usually less formal than an armistice.

Cold War: the intense rivalry after World War II between the United States (and its allies) and the Soviet Union (and its allies). The Cold War rarely "heated up" to involve armed conflict, and it ended as a result of major political changes in the Soviet Union during the 1990s.

Communism: a political and economic system in which a community or state holds all property. Some Communists in the Soviet Union and its allies wanted to destroy the capitalist system, where individuals hold property.

demarcation line: a final border drawn by agreement between opposing armies

demilitarized zone (DMZ): an area between two hostile parties where military operations are banned

dysentery: a disease of the intestines that causes bleeding and severe diarrhea

frostbite: injury to the body due to extreme cold. Frostbite usually first attacks fingers and toes, which sometimes have to be removed to prevent life-threatening infection.

napalm: a highly flammable jellylike substance used in firebombs and flamethrowers. Used to thicken gasoline, napalm is short for naphthene palmitate. U.S. soldiers first used napalm in World War II.

Soviet Union: short for the Union of Soviet Socialist Republics, or USSR, a Communist country of fifteen republics formed in 1922. One republic was Russia, the traditional name for the entire country. In 1991 several Soviet republics gained independence, and the remaining part of the USSR was renamed Russia.

Truman Doctrine: a Cold War program developed under President Harry Truman, in which the United States gave money and military aid to countries in Europe. The aim of the program was to stop the spread of Communism and the influence of the Soviet Union in Europe.

United Nations (UN): an international organization formed in 1945 by the Allies after World War II to maintain peace and stability among the nations of the world. Among other things, the UN also provides economic aid to countries in need.

WHO'S WHO?

Marguerite Higgins (1920–1966)

Marguerite Higgins, a U.S. journalist, went to South Korea in 1950 to report for the *New York Herald* on the country's elections. When North Korea attacked, she stayed to cover the story on the front lines. As she reported on the war, Higgins carried three prized possessions: a toothbrush, a box of flea powder, and a portable typewriter. In 1951 Higgins won the Pulitzer Prize for overseas reporting.

Kim Il Sung (1912–1994)

Born in Pyongyang, North Korea, as Kim Sung-ju, Kim grew up in Manchuria and fought against the Japanese. He fled to the Soviet Union in 1940 and joined the Soviet army. Kim returned to Pyongyang in 1945 and, aided by Soviet leader Joseph Stalin, became the first premier of the Democratic People's Republic of Korea in 1948. He guided the invasion of South Korea and depended heavily on the support of the Soviet Union and China. Kim led North Korea for forty-six years until his death.

Jacob Malik (1906–1980)

In 1945 Soviet-born Jacob (or Yacov) Malik, then a diplomat, wrote a report recommending that the United States and Soviet Union help Korea become an independent democracy. In 1948 Malik became the Soviet Union's ambassador to the United Nations. He pressed the UN to admit Communist China as a member, and when UN members refused, he boycotted the UN for months. During his absence, the UN voted to commit troops to defend South Korea against the Soviet-backed government in North Korea. Malik warned of China's entry into the war and worked behind the scenes for a truce. In June 1951, he used a brief radio broadcast to call for cease-fire negotiations.

Paik Sun Yup (b. 1920)

General Paik commanded South Korean forces during the Korean War. Under his able leadership, South Korean troops captured Pyongyang, the capital of North Korea, where Paik grew up. In 1952 Paik studied military operations in the United States and met with President Eisenhower. General Paik became chief of staff of the South Korean army and took part in the peace negotiations. Under the order of South Korean president Rhee, General Paik did not sign the armistice agreement.

Peng Dehai (1898–1974)

General Peng lived in poverty as a child growing up in China, then served in several armies before joining the Communists in 1927. Peng was a close ally and friend of Chinese leader Mao Zedong. Peng led Chinese troops in massive attacks against UN forces in Korea. In November 1950, he dealt the U.S. Marines their worst defeat in history. After the war ended, Peng became China's minister of defense.

Syngman Rhee (1875–1965)

Born Yi Sung-man, Rhee grew up among the elite *yangban* class in Seoul and became an English instructor. He then studied in the United States and remained there, asking for help to free Korea from Japanese rule. Rhee returned to Korea in 1945 and was elected the first president of the new republic in southern Korea in 1948. Throughout the Korean War and afterward, Rhee pressed for a united Korea. He resigned the presidency and fled to Hawaii after riots erupted in Seoul in 1960.

Matthew Ridgway (1895–1993)

A career soldier in the U.S. Army, Matthew Ridgway graduated from West Point in 1917 and later commanded U.S. troops in World War II. When General Walker died in December 1950, Ridgway took his place as leader of the Eighth Army in Korea. In April 1951, he replaced General MacArthur as supreme commander of all UN forces in Korea, and in 1952, he took over as commander of NATO.

Anna Rosenberg (1902–1983)

Born Anna Mariė Lederer in Hungary, Rosenberg emigrated to New York City with her family in 1912. She served on the War Manpower Commission in World War II. Rosenberg became an assistant secretary of defense for manpower and personnel, the highest position ever attained by a woman in the U.S. military. During the Korean War, she led programs to recruit women into the military and to improve conditions for female and African American soldiers.

Joseph Stalin (1879–1953)

Born Iosif Vissarionovich Dzhugashvili, Stalin took his name from a Russian word meaning "man of steel." He assumed control of the Russian Communist Party after the death of Vladimir Lenin and had become the head of the Soviet Union by 1929. Stalin was a ruthless leader, killing off his opposition and pushing his country toward becoming a world power. Stalin gave military supplies to the North Koreans and trained pilots during the Korean War, but China committed most of the troops. Negotiations for peace improved shortly after Stalin's death in March 1953.

Harry S. Truman (1884–1972)

Harry S. Truman was born in Missouri, where he worked on the family farm and later owned a men's clothing store. He became a U.S. senator in 1934 and vice president in 1944, succeeding to the presidency when Franklin Roosevelt died in office on April 12, 1945. World War II ended during Truman's first year in office. He was reelected for president for a second term in 1948 and went from arranging a post–World War II peace with Japan to overseeing the conflict in a divided Korea. Truman retired to private life in 1953.

SOURCE NOTES

4 Donald K. Chung, *The Three Day Promise: A Korean Soldier's Memoir* (Tallahassee, FL: Father and Son Publishing, 1989), 184.

5 Ibid.

5 Ibid., 185.

10 Ibid., 89.

13 Stanley Weintraub, *MacArthur's War: Korea and the Undoing of an American Hero* (New York: The Free Press, 2000), 21.

15 Chung, 109.

16 David Halberstam, *The Fifties* (New York: Villard Books, 1993), 73.

16 Edward F. Dolan, *America in the Korean War* (Brookfield, CT: The Millbrook Press, 1998), 18.

17 Halberstam, 70.

18 President Harry S. Truman, *Executive Order 9981: Establishing the President's Committee on Equality of Treatment and Opportunity in the Armed Services.* (Washington, D.C.: Government Printing Office, 1948).

19 David McCullough, *Truman* (New York: Simon & Schuster, 1992), 860.

20 Halberstam, 76.

21 Weintraub, 83.

25 Stanley Sandler, *The Korean War: No Victors, No Vanquished* (Lexington, KY: University Press of Kentucky, 1999), 87.

26 Edwin Simmons, *Over the Seawall: U.S. Marines at Inchon* (Washington, D.C.: History and Museums Division, U.S. Marine Corps, 2000), 27.

29 James Matray, ed., *Historical Dictionary of the Korean War* (New York: Greenwood Press, 1991), 179–180.

29 Antoinette May, *Witness to War: A Biography of Marguerite Higgins* (New York: Beaufort Books, Inc., 1983) 180.

29 Weintraub, 70.

31 Dolan, 54.

31 Weintraub, 181.

32 McCullough, 799.

33 Sandler, 103.

33 Robert Leckie, *Conflict: The History of the Korean War, 1950–1953* (New York: Da Capo Press, 1962), 161.

34 McCullough, 807.

34 Joseph H. Alexander, *Battle of the Barricades: U.S. Marines in the Recapture of Seoul* (Washington, DC: History and Museums Division, U.S. Marine Corps, 2000), 53.

36 Marc I. Leavey, *Al Jolson Society Official Website,* May 4, 2003, <http://www.jolson.org/iajs/50/50th.html> (May 8, 2003).

36 Weintraub, 219.

37 Alexander, 60.

40 Ibid., 64.

41 Chung, 95.

41 Leckie, 159.

41 Edwin P. Hoyt, *The Day the Chinese Attacked: Korea, 1950* (New York: McGraw-Hill, 1990), 80.

41 Sandler, 226.

43 Halberstam, 108.

43 Leckie, 221.

44 Sandler, 205.

45 Weintraub, 282–283.

45 McCullough, 816.

45 Robert H. Ferrell, *Harry S. Truman: A Life* (Columbia, MO: University of Missouri Press, 1994), 329.

46 Hoyt, 195.

46 Chung, 161.

46 Judith Bellafaire, curator, Women in Military Service for America Memorial Foundation, Inc., interview by author, Arlington, Virginia, May, 7, 1999.

47 Weintraub, 289.

47 Sandler, 132.

47 Leckie, 285.

50 Weintraub, 342.

50 Ibid., 343.

50–51 Leckie, 274–275.

51 Weintraub, 339.

51–52 Halberstam, 115.

52 Ibid.

53 Leckie, 289.

56 Dolan, 93.

58 Sonia G. Benson, *Korean War: Almanac and Primary Sources* (New York: U·X·L, 2002), 157.

59 Kathleen McDermott, ed. *Remembering the Forgotten War.* (New York: History Book Club, 2000), 30–31.

63 Bellafaire, interview.

64 Leckie, 326.

65 McDermott, 86–87.

67 Ibid., 358.

69 Robert Ferrell, ed., *The Eisenhower Diaries* (New York: W. W. Norton & Company, 1981), 248.

70 Benson, 262.

72 Stephen E. Ambrose, *Eisenhower: Soldier and President* (New York: Simon & Schuster, 1990), 330.

74 McDermott, 6.

74 Sandler, 214.

76 McCullough, 781.

76 Leckie, 244.

77 McDermott, 120.

77 McCullough, 936.

SELECTED BIBLIOGRAPHY, FURTHER READING, AND WEBSITES

SELECTED BIBLIOGRAPHY

Bache, Rosemary Eckroat. *Women's War Memoirs.* Waco, TX: Western Heritage Books, 1999.

Benson, Sonia G. *Korean War: Almanac and Primary Sources.* New York: U·X·L, 2002.

Bowers, William T., William M. Hammond, and George L. MacGarrigle. *Black Soldier/White Army: The 24th Infantry Regiment in Korea.* Washington, D.C.: Center for Military History, United States Army, 1996.

Buckley, Gail. *American Patriots: The Story of Blacks in the Military from the Revolution to Desert Storm.* New York: Random House, 2001.

Chung, Donald K. *The Three Day Promise: A Korean Soldier's Memoir.* Tallahassee, FL: Father and Son Publishing, 1989.

Dolan, Edward F. *America in the Korean War.* Brookfield, CT: The Millbrook Press, 1998.

Ferrell, Robert H. *Harry S. Truman: A Life.* Columbia, MO: University of Missouri Press, 1994.

Halberstam, David. *The Fifties.* New York: Villard Books, 1993.

Leckie, Robert. *Conflict: The History of the Korean War, 1950–1953.* New York: Da Capo Press, 1962.

McCullough, David. *Truman.* New York: Simon & Schuster, 1992.

McDermott, Kathleen, ed. *Remembering the Forgotten War.* New York: History Book Club, 2000.

Ridgway, Matthew B. *The Korean War.* Garden City, NY: Doubleday & Company, Inc., 1967.

Sandler, Stanley. *The Korean War: No Victors, No Vanquished.* Lexington, KY: University Press of Kentucky, 1999.

Simmons, Edwin. *Over the Seawall: U.S. Marines at Inchon.* Washington, D.C.: History and Museums Division, U.S. Marine Corps, 2000.

U. S. Department of State. *Korea: 1945 to 1948.* Washington, D.C.: U.S. Government Printing Office, 1948.

Weintraub, Stanley. *MacArthur's War: Korea and the Undoing of an American Hero.* New York: The Free Press, 2000.

FURTHER READING

Balgassi, Haemi. *Peacebound Trains.* New York: Clarion Books, 1996.

Benson, Sonia G. *Korean War: Biographies.* New York: U·X·L, 2002.

DuBois, Jill. *Korea.* New York: Marshall Cavendish, 1994.

English, June A., and Thomas D. Turner. *Encyclopedia of the United States at War.* New York: Scholastic, Inc., 1998.

Feldman, Ruth Tenzer. *The Korean War: 1950–1953. Cobblestone Magazine,* Fall, 1999.

Lazo, Caroline Evenson. *Harry S. Truman.* Minneapolis: Lerner Publications Company, 2003.

Sherman, Josepha. *The Cold War.* Minneapolis: Lerner Publications Company, 2004.

WEBSITES

"Korean War 50th Anniversary." *United States of America Korean War Commemoration.* <http://Korea50.army.mil/>

"Korean War Veterans Memorial." *National Parks Service.* <http://www.nps.gov/kwvm/

The Korean War Veterans National Museum and Library <http://www.theforgottenvictory.org/>

"State-Level Casualty Lists for the Korean Conflict," *U.S. National Archives and Records Administration.* <http://www.archives.gov/research_room/research_topics/korean_war_casualty_lists/state_level_index_alphabetical.html>
More information is available at:
National Archives and Records Administration
8601 Adelphi Road
College Park, MD 20740-6001.
email: <cer@nara.gov>

OTHER RESOURCES

Korean War: Fire and Ice. Produced by Sammy Jackson, Lou Reda Productions, Inc. 200 min. The History Channel (A&E Television Networks), 1999. Videocassette.

INDEX

ABOUT THE AUTHOR

Ruth Tenzer Feldman is an award-winning author, whose works include a biography of Thurgood Marshall, *How Congress Works,* and *Don't Whistle in School: The History of America's Public Schools.* A former attorney with the U.S. Department of Education, Ms. Feldman is also a frequent contributor to *Cobblestone* and *Odyssey* magazines. She shares her Bethesda, Maryland, home with her family, her Welsh corgi, and her trusty computer.

PHOTO ACKNOWLEDGMENTS

The images in this book are used with the permission of: © CORBIS, pp. 4–5, 36, 83 (second from top); © Bettmann/CORBIS, pp. 6, 9, 10 (bottom), 11, 12, 20, 29 (top), 33, 41, 45, 61, 71, 75, 82 (top and second from top), 83 (top and middle); National Archives, pp. 8, 17, 18, 19, 21, 22, 24, 26, 27 (top), 30, 31, 32, 34, 35, 37, 38 (top), 40, 42, 46, 47, 49, 50, 53, 59, 60, 62, 63, 65, 67, 70, 74, 83 (second from bottom and bottom); Illustrated London News, p. 10 (top); MacArthur Memorial, pp. 13, 52; © AFP/CORBIS, p. 14; © Hulton-Deutsch Collection/ CORBIS, pp. 27 (bottom), 29 (bottom), 58, 66, 72–73, 82 (middle); © Genevieve Naylor/CORBIS, p. 28; AP/Wide World Photos, pp. 38 (bottom), 69, 82 (second from bottom); U.S. National Archives Records Group 111, p. 44 (all); Library of Congress, pp. 51, 64 (LC-USZ62-100016), 76; Harry J. Lerner, p. 54 (top); Courtesy of Bert Kortegaard, pp. 54 (bottom), 55; © Hulton/Archive by Getty Images, pp. 56, 82 (bottom). Maps by Laura Westlund, pp. 7, 23, 39, 48, 57, 61, 79.

Cover photo by © Hulton/Archive by Getty Images.